LOVE YOUR CLUTTER AWAY

A STEP-BY-STEP GUIDE TO GENTLY LETTING CLUTTER GO FOR GOOD.

CARMEN KLASSEN

CONTENTS

ILLUSTRATED (OVERSIMPLIFIED) GUIDE TO DECLUTTERING

Hey, I know you're busy. And reading a decluttering book might not be as much fun as reading the latest feel-good novel. So here's the shortest possible version of the whole book. You know, just in case. Happy Decluttering! -Carmen

* * *

1. Clear a 1 foot path to the main item in the room (bed, table, sink, washing machine….)

* * *

2. Sort each item from the path one at a time into garbage, recycling, extras/donate, use it, wrong room and IDK

* * *

3. When you get to the main item/destination, do a happy dance!

Hey, however you dance, just go for it!

* * *

4. Love Yourself

* * *

* * *

5. Clear the main item by sorting each thing in it, and then wipe it/make it (if it's a bed), maybe even vacuum it!

* * *

* * *

6. Clear one foot on either side of the main item

* * *

* * *

7. Clear the rest of the floor, beginning with the 1 foot path and extending in in a counter clockwise direction. Sort each item into garbage, recycling, extras/donate, illegal tenants, use it, wrong room and IDK.

* * *

* * *

8. Love yourself

* * *

* * *

9. One at a time, clear each surface/piece of furniture by sorting all the items, wiping down the furniture, and then putting back on it things that are used nearly every day, and a few nice things to look at.

* * *

* * *

10. When the room is clear, take all the boxes of sorted items and put them where they belong. If you can't fit them, re-sort the space where they belong, removing old/unusable/unwanted items until you can easily put away the things you use.

* * *

* * *

11. Keep each room easy to manage by following the one-in-one-out rule. You've worked so hard to love your clutter away, so make sure that clutter stays away!

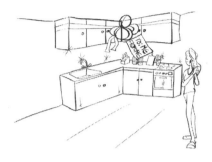

* * *

INTRODUCTION

It's been my honor to step into the homes of all sorts of clutterers and work with them as they declutter. But I've always felt a bit frustrated that I couldn't help more people. (That, and my husband kept nagging me to write a book to share what was working so well!) So here we are. This book will give you the tools to have less clutter and feel good—at the same time! It's possible, and it can change your life.

Please note: If you're reading this book because you want to encourage someone else to deal with their clutter, *please be careful*. Although it's great to want to help a loved one, what you do and say to a clutterer can make their situation much worse. Instead, use this book as an intro to how you can *love* and *support* the person who is trying to deal with their clutter. This is the most important thing you can do.

Thank you for reading! If you find the book helpful, please leave a review.

Carmen

THINGS THAT DON'T WORK

Throughout this book, I'll use the term clutterers—never hoarders. While hoarding has certainly become a household term, it's a clinical diagnosis and should be treated by qualified, caring mental health experts. If you think you're a hoarder this book *will* help you. But you deserve to have an individualized mental health plan as well. Please ask your doctor, call helplines, talk to a counselor, and keep on asking until you find the support you need to live a happy, healthy, safe life. You may be a hoarder, but you're also an interesting, valuable *person*. As my late father used to say, "we've all got a can of worms." Yours just happens to include lots of clutter.

Let's start with what *doesn't* work for getting rid of clutter—and we'll give those the heave ho.

1. Reading books about how to declutter. If you only read books and don't take action, then the books have only enabled you to hide from your clutter for a while. Even this book won't help you if all you do is read it.

2. Attending support groups, conferences, and workshops. All the information in the world will not help *unless* you go home

and put that support and information to work getting rid of clutter.

3. Watching TV programs about hoarders. While there is some good being done while the cameras roll, this is *not* the way to declutter. Most of those shows highlight the worst of the worst, put hoarders under immense pressure, and sensationalize a very real mental illness in a way that invites judgement and condemnation from the general public. (If you live in the UK however, there are some good shows that demonstrate help and progress over time, and are doing really good work.)

4. Comparing yourself to others. If you are constantly looking at your very organized friend's home and comparing it to yours, please stop. You're not them. They're not you. You cannot justify keeping things just because someone you know who's nearly clutter-free is keeping those same things. You're not them.

Taking clutter out the front door as fast as you're bringing it in the back door. If the amount going out equals the amount coming in, then you are not getting ahead. This includes buying books, organizing supplies, bags, sticky notes, and anything else that you plan to use one day when you declutter.

If you've used these methods in the past, DO NOT get all angry at yourself! You *were* trying, and that's really important. Instead of regret about the past, I would like you to love the person you were in the past. Think back to that person who was trying to make a change in their life, and allow yourself to love that person. You may even feel compassion for yourself and all that you were going through. Warning: do not get caught in a pity party when you do this! Compassion is about experiencing care for the person you were, pity is seeing yourself as a victim and blaming others for your circumstances. There is *no* blame in any method of trying to clear your clutter. You are who you are now. You were who you were then.

As you may already know, clutterers have so much because they're way better at getting things than they are at getting rid of things. Letting something go often makes them feel scared, anxious, wasteful, ungrateful, mean, exhausted and hopeless. So, it's not hard to see why clutterers hang on to things—who wants to feel *that* crappy just to get rid of something?!?

(Neat freaks have a hard time with this. That's because they *love* the feeling of purging their stuff, and have a hard time seeing life a different way. But for clutterers it's often very distressing to even think about getting rid of some of their things.)

At the risk of sounding lame, "the first step to solving a problem is admitting you have a problem." So, well done! The most obvious part of your problem is that you have too much stuff (I know you know this but bear with me). But from my experience, this is rarely the *real* problem.

If you wanted to get to the root of it all you would need to understand *why* you have accumulated so much, *where* the clutter came from, and *how* to change your habits so you can get rid of some things. The great news is that you don't actually have to get to the root of the *why* and the *where* to find success! For some of you this will be a great relief, because you really don't want to revisit your past. There will be times, as you declutter, that your past will need dealing with, but you don't have to face every skeleton in your closet before you can make some room in there!

However, I *know* there are others out there that are a bit disappointed by this. You'd rather sit with a workbook and analyze yourself and your situation until the cows come home—and avoid tackling your clutter! The thing is, the only way to start to have less clutter is to start to take things out of your house. And if you spend all your time reading and analyzing yourself you're not actually changing your situation.

THE SOLUTION IS YOURS TODAY!

So, what helps clutterers feel better and live better?

It all starts with a little bit of love. (Is it time to cue some touchy-feely music yet?)

Nope, I'm not crazy. Think about it. How do you feel when you look at your clutter? How have other people made you feel? What messages have you been given about your clutter? Maybe you've been told that you're lazy, a slob, good for nothing, or inconsiderate. You don't get many positive messages as a clutterer. You may love your clutter, but you don't love yourself. Sadly, your clutter doesn't love you either.

So let's bring the focus onto you and not your clutter for the moment. You matter. You *are* important. You have many good things to offer the world. You Are Loved. You. Not 'you and your clutter', just you. That's what's important. Keep the focus on yourself for a moment, and begin to give yourself the love you need. Sounds a bit too far out there for you? It works! I know personally that it works. When you start to love yourself you start to *feel* loved from the very inside of you. So love yourself. Say it out loud, 'I love myself'. Repeat it over and over for 3 minutes, and imagine love growing inside of you like warmth, comfort, and caring.

Keep on loving you. If you want to go all out, and really get the most out of life then stop reading this book (just for now). Purchase a copy of *Love Yourself Like Your Life Depends On It*, read it through (it's a quick read), and do what it says. It will change your life!!

It's quite amazing to see what happens when you really try to love yourself. In my experience, life just starts to feel better. I promise that as you tell yourself over and over 'I love myself' and really give yourself a chance to mean it and feel it, your life *will* be better.

If your loved one/roommate/friend is a clutterer, and you are critical, unkind, or constantly negative to them and about their clutter, they will have a MUCH harder time letting things go. The more that negative emotions are stirred up, the stronger a clutterer will hang on to their clutter. So, if you want to be helpful, start by loving them. Find all the good things about them that don't have to do with their clutter, and consistently support and encourage them in those aspects of their life. Did they take out a bag of garbage? Don't mumble, "It's about time you started cleaning up." Thank them acknowledge their action, and then tell them from the heart that you love them.

If you constantly berate yourself about your clutter, it makes it much harder for you to declutter. Once you start to really experience loving yourself, you can begin to deal with your clutter successfully. Start loving yourself, and then *keep* loving yourself as you start to declutter.

There's something about you and the things in your life that has pushed you to read this book. First of all, you get a high five from me for getting this far into the book! Yay you!! Many people buy clutter books and never read them, but *you* are still reading, and I thank you for that.

Second, if you are feeling *any* negative emotions right now, please take 3 minutes to sit quietly and repeat 'I love myself'. Really focus on meaning what you are saying, even if you don't feel like you should love yourself yet.

Done 3 minutes? Thank you! Loving yourself is the best place to be!

Now, look up from your reading, and look around your space (if you're not at home, try to picture your space, or check out any pictures of your home you have on your phone). What do you feel? The environment you live in is either uplifting or it's not. There's no neutral here. Clutter generates a lot of negative feelings. It reminds you of things you haven't done, stuff you spent valuable money on, sadness from your past, projects you said you would do, and decisions that need to be made.

If you can't look around your home and smile, then your clutter is a problem. Even if you really love everything around you, keep reading this book and see what inspires you.

Another warning: clutterers have this interesting skill—they can see other people's clutter *much* easier than they can see their own. So if you looked around your room and got upset about someone else's clutter—try again. But this time refuse to look at the clutter that's not yours. Your stuff is there, trust me.

So again, here's the "secret" to this whole book. Focus first on loving yourself. Even if it seems really silly at first, keep saying 'I love myself'. Say it when you fall asleep, say it when you wake up, say it during your commute, during commercials, and any time that thoughts about your clutter crop up. I'll walk you through each step of having less clutter in your home—and there will be lots of loving yourself for the whole book. Aside from the cost of this book, *nothing* in the book will require you to spend more money. The potential to love yourself is already inside of you—you just need to let it grow. As you do, everything is going to start changing for the better.

Are you on board with having your home make you feel happy and peaceful? Yay! Let's get started.

THE BEST WAY TO DECLUTTER

An attitude of loving yourself combined with the actions we'll cover in the rest of this book will create magic in your space and your life (OK, "magic" may be pushing it, but only by a little bit!) Here's the strategy:

1. Love yourself
2. Consistently remove things from your environment(s) until much of the clutter is gone
3. Find ways to love yourself that have nothing to do with clutter

If you've been struggling with clutter for most of your life, these three steps may seem absolutely ridiculous. As someone who has spent years helping people get rid of clutter, I can understand how silly it may seem to take such a complex issue and give it a three-step process. But my experience has shown that the best way to get rid of clutter and keep it gone is to find out the good person you are while you let go of the clutter (and self-hatred) that's been messing up your life.

Let's focus on Step 1: Love Yourself. This provides many benefits at once. To begin with, you start to feel more positive when you focus on loving yourself. The truth is, we were *made* to be loved. Loving and being loved are some of the best parts of human nature. So when you love yourself you are meeting a basic human need. And since most of you began to accumulate clutter in response to unmet needs and desires, loving yourself is the perfect place to begin filling that need with something good.

Another reason to love yourself when you clear clutter is that it helps to create new wiring in your brain. For many years (maybe even your entire life), getting rid of clutter hasn't felt very good. You may have even experienced severe trauma related to losing your belongings. There are many clutterers I know that experienced a sudden, devastating loss of things they cared deeply about. As a result, their brains learned that getting rid of things is bad, upsetting, stressful, and even wrong. If you're in the same situation, you need to retrain your brain so that getting rid of clutter becomes easier.

Right now, getting rid of clutter is hard to do. So take the time to love yourself every time you make an item leave your house. Tell yourself out loud *'I love myself'* and visualize yourself smiling proudly at yourself. Did you get that? Encouraging words, a happy tone, and a proud response, help train your brain. At every step I give you for the rest of this book, be sure you are genuinely rewarding yourself in words, tone, and response. Because this is hard. But you are doing it, and that's awesome!

Beginning in the next chapter, you'll be loving the clutter away one space/room at a time. Each chapter will walk you through every step, and tell you what to do with the things you come across. Please read the whole chapter through first once, and then read it through again while you get started on loving your clutter away. This book will give you the best results when you work while you read, so have a read of the next chapter and then get started.

WARMING UP

Clutterers always ask me, "Where do I start?" So if you're wondering where to begin, you're in good company! You need to start somewhere that will leave you feeling successful. Choose somewhere small, and somewhere you will see every day. Since everyone's circumstances are different, 'small' will have a different meaning. The more clutter you have, the smaller your small will be.

So, if you have rooms of your home that are unusable due to clutter, or if you can't see your dining room table, or if your car is so full you have to move things to get in, or something similar, then your small needs to be really small. About 1 foot by 1 foot. This can be the space on your bedside table, an area on your couch, a place at your table, the dash of your car, etc.

If clutter is not quite as pervasive, your 'small' can be bigger. It can be your dining room table, the front hallway, or maybe the space around your bed.

In either situation, choose somewhere that you see every day. Your goal is to create and keep a clutter-free space. Before you start creating this clutter-free space, read through the chapter and picture yourself going through each step. Just make sure you do the 'I love myself' portions in full – it will give you a great start! Then, come back to this point, and do each step.

Here's how you start:

1. Love yourself out loud for a minute. Breathe deeply and slowly as you do this. Then get a bag for **garbage**. Find anything you can easily grab that is garbage, and put it in the bag. Keep the bag handy as you work through the rest of the steps, and put any more garbage you find in it as you go.

2. Think about how you're feeling. If you feel at all anxious or stressed, love yourself out loud and breathe deeply and slowly for at least a minute. The process of loving yourself is the most important part of your journey, so take your time with this. Then get a bag/container for **recycling**. Use the same process – find anything you can easily grab that's recycling and put it in the bag. Often this will include flyers, paper and plastic containers (look for the recycling symbol on the bottom of the container ♻, if it's there you can recycle it.) If you aren't sure about something just leave it there. Only grab the things you can easily decide are recycling.

3. Next, grab the things that belong in your home – but are in the wrong place. These are called **Wrong Room**, and will go in a box/bag with a label that says Wrong Room. This is a really common clutter category, because it's hard to put things away when your house is full. So we start by gathering the things that are in the wrong room. Later on when there's space in your home I'll help you put them away.

TIP #4 When you feel like you can't keep on going (or just really don't want to) find something in your space that belongs somewhere else, and get up and take it there.

TIP #5 When you are returning an item to its home (or closer to its home if you can't get all the way there) do not stop, do not pass go, but go <u>straight back</u> to where you were working. The *only* space you are working on right now is the small space you have chosen.

If you're comfortable where you are, all you need to do for now is collect them and put them in a clearly labelled box/bag.

4. Now, look for anything you can **donate**, and put it in a bag/box. If you'd like you can even take these things right to a donation point when you're done clearing your small space. Just follow these tips for donating:

TIP #1 If you are donating things at a thrift store or charity shop *do not* go in and look around. *Do not* put a single thing back in your vehicle. Make this a rule that you always follow.

TIP #2 Don't wait until you have 'enough' or a full load of anything you're getting rid of. You will be more successful getting 3 things gone this week than saving 200 things to get rid of next year.

5. It's time for **paperwork** (Insert scary music)! Did you know that the Number 1 clutter problem is paperwork? If you are overwhelmed with paperwork you are not alone! Of course, you can skip this step entirely if your space doesn't have any paperwork. But give this a read through so you'll be ready when you do face your paper tigers.

TIP #3 When you come across paperwork, your main task is to separate the urgent from the mountain(s). Urgent means you must deal with it or face serious consequences. Bills are urgent. Coupons are not urgent. Legal summons are urgent. Newsletters are not urgent, and so on. Place the urgent items in a visible container (something you can easily pick out of any pile) that will ONLY hold urgent paperwork. Place the rest of the paperwork in a box labelled 'papers' or something similar that makes sense to you. (Don't worry, I'll help you out with all that paperwork later in the book.)

If you want to toss/recycle things as you look for your urgent papers feel free to do this, but ONLY if it's things you can make quick decisions on. If you find yourself struggling or getting bogged down, then just focus on finding the urgent papers.

Did you find something absolutely critical that you can quickly take care of? Maybe a tax bill, or a final notice? Go ahead and take care of it, then make a note on the paper of what you've done, and then put it into the general paper box.

Once you've gone through all the papers in your small space you deserve congratulations. Congratulations!! You have started to deal with a big tricky part of the world's clutter!! Now, congratulate yourself!! And take a few minutes to love yourself. You are teaching your brain that dealing with this is a good thing.

How are you doing? Let's take a few minutes to love yourself. Remember to breathe deeply, and focus on just the words 'I love myself'. Well done!

You probably have some things in your small space that actually belong in the room you're working in. These are in a category called **Use It**. If these have a home you can get at in the room, go ahead and put them away. However, most of the time these are out for a reason – you *can't* put them away. So put them in a bag/box labelled Use It, and keep it handy.

Find everything in your small space that belongs in the room you're working in and put it here.

Still have stuff? That's OK! You're learning some great decluttering skills, and putting them to use, so keep at it!

Now, are you keeping things for other people? These things are also illegal tenants, but they can be hard to get rid of. The first thing to do is to ask that person if they want the thing(s) you're keeping for them. If you have no way of contacting them, you have no business keeping stuff for them. Please free your space from obligations you have created to people that are not actively in your life.

If you can contact this person and they don't want what you're saving, then it's time for those things to leave your life. This may be hard. Love yourself, love yourself, love yourself! You are NOT a good person because you save stuff for others. You ARE a good person because you tend to consider others as you go about your day. There's a big difference between the two, and only the second one will help you create a comfortable, inviting space in your home.

Tip #7 ASK PEOPLE if they want things you've been keeping for them, and respect them if they don't. You do not become more valuable by saving things others might want. You learn to value yourself by loving yourself.

But what do you do if they want the thing(s) you're saving for them? It's time to flex your 'self respect' muscle here. Tell them, "I'm having trouble with too many things in my house, and I can't keep this here any longer. What's the best way for you to collect this item?" If they ask you to hold onto it you can agree, but only for a very short amount of time (I'm talking days here, not months!). Be clear that you will get rid of it after that time, and follow through if they don't collect it.

Tip #8 Retraining other people. Some people in your life may be used to viewing you as their free storage unit – or a free source for anything they might need at any time. You will need to retrain them, just like you are retraining yourself! Let them know you are changing how you manage the house, and can no longer store their things. If they care enough about their things, they'll arrange to collect them.

Tip #9 Stuck with strange items you don't know what to do with? If you have things you absolutely don't know what to do with, you can get a little creative. Maybe post on Facebook and ask where it should go, or if anyone wants it. Or, write a sticky note that says **IDK**, WTF, or even just a big '?', and come back to the item another time. You may be surprised how a little bit of time makes the right choice clear.

Whoa... check out your cleared small space. You're fantastic!! Love yourself a whole bunch because this is a big deal!! Take a cloth/wipe and give your clear space a little shine up. Doesn't that look nice?

Now take the garbage and recycling you've gathered and put them where they belong. Select a space for your donate, wrong room, and paperwork boxes – you'll be adding to these as you continue the process of decluttering. (It might be tricky to find space for these at the start. Do your best, and don't worry, because from now on you're going to make more space to work with, and soon the things in those boxes will be in their proper home!) Put your 'use it' box near your clear space – you'll add to this when you finish clearing this are later.

Tip #6 Watch out for the rest of the world. When you've cleared a small space, *you* know you've done a great thing, and *I* know you've done a great thing, but the rest of the world doesn't know. If you share your home with others, they probably won't be impressed with your new, clear small space. They might even be a bit of a downer. But you <u>know</u> it's a big deal, and you *must* congratulate yourself and keep on going!

Now you've made a clear small space – congratulations!! Give the surface a wipe to shine it up. If it's obvious where the boundaries of your clear space are (such as a bedside table or seat in your car), that's great. If it's part of a bigger space (such as a part of your dining table) you need to clearly mark off your space. Best choice is tape that is a contrast to the color of your table. Mark your borders with tape, and you've got your first clear space!

Feel free to use and enjoy this beautiful clear space. BUT, as soon as you are done, clear it completely by putting the items you used away where they belong. This is now your new and improved space. For a double bonus, repeat 'I love myself' as you clear off your small space. Lucky you – you love yourself *and* you've created a clear space!! Well done!!

THE PROJECT FOR ONGOING SUCCESS

You've done your warm-up, and are keeping your small space clear and shiny. Now you get to add to your skills with an essential part of large scale decluttering. It's really the ins and outs of the whole thing…. the entrance to your home!

Here's the goal: To be able to easily walk from your parked car (or the street) right into your house without any hopping over stuff, tripping, or wiggling around things. It includes being able to open your front door <u>all the way</u>. Can you already to this? Great! Keep it that way, and hop on over to Chapter 7. If not, let's keep going.

Here's why this is important:

What you see and feel in your home (and entrance) has an impact on your decluttering success. If you can't open your front door easily, then you've created resistance to things leaving your home. (Strangely, it has *no* impact on being able to bring things into the home!) When you clear the space to, and into, your home you are giving yourself permission to take out the negative, *and* welcome the positive into your home and life.

Here's why this may be hard:

The stuff is there because you want it! Or the stuff is there because you need it *in* your house but can't get it there. Or the stuff is there because you intend to get rid of it, but just can't seem to get it all the way out the door.

How to start:

1. Take three minutes to breathe deeply and say 'I love myself'. Really focus on those words, and picture love filling you from the inside.

2. Next, look for any large things along the pathway and through your front door that you had already decided to **donate**. (This can include bags on the front porch that are waiting to leave the house.) I hear that objection: You want to hold off until you've gathered more stuff and then it can all go out together! Dear friend, please don't wait! Honor your past decisions about getting rid of things, and send them off! Remember:

TIP #2 Don't wait until you have 'enough' or a full load of anything you're getting rid of. You will be more successful getting 3 things gone this week than saving 200 things to get rid of next year.

So, go ahead and gather up anything that's to be donated. You can even take a trip and get it gone right away. You're honoring a choice you've already made, *and* starting to clear, so this is a valuable action to take.

3. Next step: **recycling**, including cardboard boxes and excess bags. Lots of people tend to collect cardboard and bags near their front door. So, you're not alone! If you don't have any good boxes in the house that are easy to carry, then set aside 5 or 6 for use while you're sorting. Flatten the rest of the cardboard boxes, and get it all to recycling so it has a chance to be useful again. Keep one bag of bags in a practical spot, and get rid of the rest. Remember to walk all the way

down to your car, looking for cardboard and bags in the path, and then cleaning them up.

4. Are you doing OK? If you're taking action, but struggling, remember the rule: Love yourself first! Stop, close your eyes, and repeat 'I love myself'. Picture good love just pouring into you and making everything peaceful. Do this for a few minutes – or longer if you want. You're working on two things right now; loving yourself, and taking action about your clutter. It isn't easy to do, so be patient with yourself.

5. Now it's time to find **garbage**. If you've had garbage building up outside your home, then your neighbors are going to *love* this step! Don't get worked up about them though. This journey is really about you, and if it makes them happy too then good for YOU!! (Cause I only care about you. I don't care about your neighbor at all!)

Start with the garbage you can pick up yourself. Every time you clear a space, take a minute to look at it and appreciate what you see. YOU are improving the environment, your yard, and the whole neighborhood by doing this, and you can feel *very* proud of what you're doing. Keep it up, and then be fiercely protective of your garbage free path. Go out of your way to remove any garbage that might get into your space. The cleaner you keep it the cleaner it will stay.

If there are large things you can't move yourself, you'll need some help. Start with anyone who's offered to help in the past. Be specific in your request: "Can you help me with getting rid of the toilet on my sidewalk? I know there are other things around, but I want to start with only the toilet for now."

You can also call your local disposal removal company, and ask around for suggestions. At this point your only jobs are:

- Love yourself

- Keep your small space clean (that space you worked on in the previous chapter)
- Remove the garbage along your entry way

(I know that's not true – you have other things in your life that are demanding your time and attention. But as far as decluttering goes, I want you to only focus on those three things.)

6. Love yourself, love yourself, love yourself! Now, take a look at your entry way. Are there things there that you are keeping for others? Remember your tips from the last chapter:

Tip #7 ASK PEOPLE if they want things you've been keeping for them, and respect them if they don't. You do not become more valuable by hoarding things others might want. You learn to value yourself by loving yourself.

And...

Tip #8 Retraining other people. Some people in your life may be used to viewing you as their free storage unit. You will need to retrain them, just like you are retraining yourself! Let them know you are changing how you manage the house, and can no longer store their things. If they care enough about their things, they'll arrange to collect them.

When you do ask people if they want the thing you're keeping, be clear with them that you are having a hard time with clutter. Sometime people think they're helping you if they say they want something (but they don't actually want it!) When they understand that you're not going to be disappointed if they say no, they'll be more honest with you. If you're keeping things for people that they don't want, you can let them go now.

7. Think about what you *need* by your front entrance. The less the better, and I'll save you from hearing the lecture about want vs need. Are there things that should somewhere else?

Throughout the book we'll call those **wrong room** items. Take them to, or near their homes. And maybe feel free to have a laugh once in a while at the things you've been allowing to take up this valuable space. Hey, you're human, not perfect!

8. Look for everything along the path and the entry that you can **donate**, and donate them. Remember the donating tips:

TIP #1 If you are donating things at a thrift store or charity shop *do not* go in and look around. *Do not* put a single thing back in your care. Make this a rule that you always follow.

TIP #2 Don't wait until you have 'enough' or a full load of anything you're getting rid of. You will be more successful getting 3 things gone this week than saving 200 things to get rid of next year. Love yourself A LOT while you recall everything you've done to get to this point.

9. If there are still things in your way, see if you can move things so that you have a safe, clear pathway. You don't need things to be perfect, just moved so the path to, and into your home is clear.

And then take a look around – you've done it! You've set yourself up so you can take the clutter *out* of your house, and let all the *good vibes in*!! YAY!! Really, this is a BIG deal!!

Now, here's the icing on the cake for this very important project you've just done:

Walk up to your house and in the door saying/singing/yelling "freedom and happiness!" Think of the feelings and love that you want coming right into your home with you.

Then walk back out of your house saying/singing/yelling "outta here!" and picture guilt, worry, and stuff that makes you sad flying right out of your home. Repeat the in and out process as many times as you want! (Feel free to wave to the neighbors too, they are *really* confused right now...)

Now that you've cleared, and christened your entryway you must protect this space as an important part of your life. Keep it clear and talk to it often. (If you've just read through this chapter for the first time, now you get to go back and find out what it really feels like to easily get in and out of your house. Go for it! I'll be here with you every step.)

GETTING YOUR WIGGLES OUT

Hey! You're still here! Thanks for reading! I hope that you've taken the steps listed so far in loving your clutter away. If you haven't, don't feel bad. Just put down this book and go do some of the steps. I know it's hard, but it *will* get easier as you focus on loving yourself and taking action! Here's a reason to come right back after you've taken action – this is a <u>short</u> chapter.

Alright, so now you've been practicing loving yourself. You've got a small space that you've been using and keeping clear, you can easily get into your home (bringing all those good vibes with you), and you can easily carry clutter out of your home (taking all those crappy vibes away for good).

Are you ready for a little wander through your house? First, set a timer for 3 minutes, get comfortable, and repeat with meaning 'I love myself'.

Now, find a bag that can hold some garbage. Start at the front door of your home, and do your best to make a counter clockwise trip through every room of your home, picking up garbage until the bag is full. If you really hate being told what to do, maybe travel clockwise instead. (It doesn't actually matter, I just have a picture in my head of you going counter clockwise so I'm working with it!)

When the bag is full, take it to wherever **garbage** belongs. If you want, you can keep on doing this until you've made it through the whole house. If you don't want to that's OK. You've done a whole bag, and you're almost done with this chapter already!

Next, get a bag/box suitable for collecting **recycling**. Make another trip through your house collecting all recyclables until the box is full. Take it to where the recycling goes, and sort if required. Repeat as many times as you want. This process is called 'Getting Your Wiggles Out'. When you have a day where you just don't want to focus on one project, or when you feel you've been stuck in one area for way too long, you can take a break and do this instead.

What's so special about this? Not much really. It's just that decluttering can be really hard, and if you've been stuck working on the same area for a long time, then it can get tiring and discouraging. Giving yourself a change of scenery – even if it's just for 10 minutes – while still making progress is a great solution for decluttering fatigue. I hope it helped you!

REFLECTIONS OF A CLUTTER FREE LIFE

Up next is everyone's least favorite place to clean – the bathroom! OK, I know not everyone hates it, but I'm pretty sure it's a majority thing. Cleaning your bathroom gives you a respectable space where you can make yourself respectable every morning! Yes, I know you clean up well even when you have to balance your toothbrush on top of the jar that's on top of the book that's on top of a mash of other things on your counter. But your life will be easier (and maybe happier!) when you can take care of yourself without the balancing act.

NOTE: If your bathroom is really full of clutter, this may not be a job you can complete quickly. Start a timer, and see how long you can work at your bathroom. Note the time, and when you work on your bathroom again the next day, add 10 minutes to your max time and go for it! Repeat each day, increasing your time each day until you're done. On average, when I've worked with a client to declutter their bathroom (no cleaning) it takes about three hours. So if you're flying solo here, understand that this is a big job, and you're really going to have to stick to it in order to get it done. You *can* do it!!

Choose the bathroom you most often use to get ready in the morning. First place to start? Loving yourself, of course. Give yourself three minutes to say 'I love myself.'

Next up is the mirror. So gather whatever you use to clean your mirror (or whatever you *would* use *if* you cleaned your mirror) and get started. You may not be able to access the entire mirror yet, so just clean what you can. If there's a lot of build-up on the glass you can get most of it off with a cloth before doing the proper mirror cleaning bit. Get it nice and shiny. Clean it twice or three times if you need to. Now look at yourself in the mirror. Look right into your eye and say out loud 'I love myself'. Look into your other eye and say out loud 'I love myself'. Add this practice into your day – the more often the better! (And now you know why it's such a good idea to keep your mirror clean!)

Next? Put the toilet seat down. Please. It's such a pain to fish things out of the toilet when you're trying to declutter and you drop something!

TIP #10 At any time if you are feeling like you just can't do anymore, remember that it's OK to stop. You're doing something that's very different than what you're used to and it can take some time to get in the groove. Always end a loving your clutter away session by taking three minutes to say 'I love myself' out loud. Then, make sure the area you were working on is left safe, take all your sorted categories to their homes, and give yourself a well-deserved break!

Now get yourself a **garbage** bag and a **recycling** bag. Start with the garbage. Collect everything you can reach that's garbage and toss it. Repeat this process with recyclables.

Alright, take a minute (an actual 60 second minute), and look at yourself in the mirror while you repeat 'I love myself'. Feeling good? Well I'm feeling good for you! Because tackling the bathroom is a big deal, and here you are doing it! (You are doing it, right?)

Next, get *another* bag or box for give away/donate. I'm going to give you a really good rule here:

<u>GOOD RULE</u>: For every bathroom/beauty/personal care product, only keep one extra.

This means you could have a bottle of moisture cream that you're using, and one extra. That's it. Oh, and not one extra in every scent! Just one extra. Some of you are feeling a bit upset right now. Because you have *way* more than just one extra, and you know I'm going to ask you to get rid of them. (It's true, I am)

Fortunately, there are some places that would really appreciate your extra extras if you don't want to put them in the trash. Shelters, halfway houses, and even food banks can give your extra extras to needy people. And that's a really good thing! The only thing you must do is check that they're not expired. DO NOT donate expired things!!! Don't Don't Don't. Please. It is really degrading when you are in need and you receive an item that wouldn't be put on a shelf for a regular person.

Tip #9 – It's good to donate, but only donate good stuff!

OK, back to bathroom talk. Phew! So here's what you do next:

1. Start to take things off your bathroom counter one at a time. Sort them into garbage, recycling, extras, wrong room (for things you need that don't belong in the bathroom) or use it. Just keep going one thing at a time. When you fill a bag, get up, take it to where it belongs, and make sure to tell yourself how very impressive it is that you have just removed a *bagful* of clutter from your bathroom! Then come right back to the bathroom counter.

Remember the <u>GOOD RULE</u>: For every bathroom/beauty/personal care product, only keep one extra.

2. When you find your counter, do a little dance, and get a cloth and some cleaner and scrub that counter like you're being paid big money to do it! Once it's nice and shiny and

clean, put back on it the things you use <u>every</u> day that you'd like to keep out.

Next, move to the back of the toilet. Repeat the same process as the counter: sort into garbage, recycling, extras, wrong room or use it. Remember the <u>GOOD RULE: For every bathroom/beauty/personal care product, only keep one extra.</u>

3. When the surface is clear, clean it. But the only thing you can put back on it is a spare roll or two of toilet paper. (The only exception is if you don't actually have any counter space. Then you'll need to use the back of the toilet for a few items you use <u>every</u> day, and that's OK.)

4. Now it's time to clear the floor. Again, sort every item into garbage, recycling, extras, wrong room or use it. If your wrong room bag/box gets full, grab a paper, write 'WRONG ROOM – FROM BATHROOM' on it, and try to place it near your paperwork boxes from your first decluttering step.

TIP #11 – Every time you set aside a box of things you've sorted, label it clearly with a label that is certain to stay with the box. That way, when you come across it again you'll remember what it is and where it came from. You'll be surprised how much duplicate sorting this little task will save you!

5. Take a break. Go get a drink or a small snack, get a breath of fresh air, maybe do some stretches. Don't check Facebook – you may fall down the Facebook rabbit hole of infinite time and be lost to your most important task (decluttering the bathroom). Set a timer for 3 minutes and repeat 'I love myself' over and over with meaning.

6. Take a look at the bathroom floor. Here's the things that can stay on the floor:

- Plunger
- Extra rolls of toilet paper (best if they are neatly kept on a holder or in a small container).
- A clothes hamper for dirty clothes if you tend to change in your bathroom, and if you have room for it.

That's all folks! I know it can be a big change not to keep other things around on the bathroom floor. I mean, it's space, right? So you can put things there, right? Nope. Sometimes space is meant to just be space.

> 7. This is so exciting! You've almost cleared the entire bathroom!! Next step is the bathtub/shower area.

Let's assume for a minute that it's so full of clutter you don't actually use it for anything except storage. This is one of the warning signs for hoarding disorder: being unable to use certain spaces in your home for their intended purpose. Even if you have another shower/bathtub you use, it is *not* OK to fill this space with clutter. BUT if it is full, I'm going to ask you to only take the garbage and recycling that you can reach out of it, and leave the rest for now. Because if your bathtub is full, then so is the rest of your home and you have no place to put anything that's in it if you were to declutter it.

If you are not using your bathtub for storage, go ahead and tackle it using the same method as the counter, toilet, and floor: sort into garbage, recycling, extras, wrong room or use it. When a bag/box gets full, take it away. Remember to label any bag/box of things you are keeping for future reference. Keep following the GOOD RULE: For every bathroom/beauty/personal care product, only keep one extra.

Now, here's where you get to burn some calories! It's time to give another excellent cleaning to your bathtub/shower. Here are my two favorite methods for this really tough job:

- Rinse out the entire area to wash down the loose gunk.

Then, use a Mr. Clean magic eraser for the bathroom. Starting as high as you can reach, scrub each area until it is shiny. Every little while make sure to rinse everything down so it doesn't dry back on. When you're finished, dry the faucet and taps with a cloth so they're nice and bright.

- Hire someone with experience to clean it for you.

8. This final step is what set's you up to keep your bathroom uncluttered: tackling the storage areas. This may include a medicine cabinet, drawers, and shelves. Start with the highest point closest to the mirror and then work your way down and around. Now that you know what's next, take 3 minutes to love yourself.

You'll be using the same basic method as you take each item out. Sort into garbage, recycling, extras, wrong room or use it. Remember the GOOD RULE: For every bathroom/beauty/personal care product, only keep one extra.

In order to be able to put things away that you will use, you have to really get rid of a lot of stuff during this time. Here are some more rules to help you:

- Get rid of all expired prescription medicines. For now, put them all into a zipper bag labelled 'EXPIRED MEDS'. When you have finished the bathroom, dispose of them safely. Your best choices are your local police station (which may have a collection box), or your pharmacist who may belong to a program that can safely dispose of them.
- It's been suggested that expired over-the-counter medicines like Tylenol and Aspirin are still OK to use, only less potent. But really, if the bottle expired anytime before the year 2000 there is *no way* you're going to finish it in this lifetime! Put them in with the expired meds, and create some space for the life you are living right now.
- Creams, shampoos, ointments – anything like a thick liquid

– will separate over time. Throw out anything expired, and anything that is a different color than when you bought it.

TIP #12 – Things that have been taking up space in your home for so long that they have changed color/quality have overstayed their welcome and are clutter, not useful. Throw them out.

- If mascara or makeup has an odor throw it out. The odor is caused by bacteria that you should not be putting on your face.
- Keep makeup you use every day, and one set of special occasion makeup. Throw the rest out.
- How often do you paint your nails in a month? This number plus 3 is the amount of nail polishes you could have.
- Anytime you find something that makes you feel angry for keeping it, stop. Remind yourself that you love yourself now, and that the actions you took in the past were simply part of your journey. Love yourself, toss the item, and move on.
- Once you've cleared out a section. Replace the things you want to keep. If there isn't some free space in every shelf and drawer then you'll need to repeat the steps and get rid of more things. (And that free space is not an invitation to buy more products. It's free space that helps you easily put away your things so they don't become clutter).
- Repeat for each section.

OK, if you've made it this far and completed each step you must be very very proud of yourself!! I can't emphasize enough what a lifestyle change you're making, and how amazing it is that you're doing this! I estimate that at least one house on every block in North America is overwhelmed with clutter. Each of those dear souls is struggling with more than they can manage. And here you are, making amazing progress and clearing out the clutter!!!!!! Congratulations!!!!!

VISITING OLD FRIENDS

One of the (many) hard things about decluttering is about keeping spaces clear as you continue to declutter. Can you believe how much you've done since you started loving your clutter away? You'd better stop and love yourself for 3 minutes to reinforce how awesome you are! Let's go back to the places you've already worked on. Start with your small space. How's it looking? If it's clear, pat yourself on the back, and head to your entryway.

If it's got some clutter on it, that's OK! You're a work in progress, just like everyone else. And when you're a clutterer, there's a lot of work and effort involved as you make progress. Before you touch anything in your small space, take a look.

Where did the items come from?

- If they're garbage, why didn't you take them to the garbage? You might answer that you're just lazy. Well, that's negative so let's not go there. If you *could* have taken the garbage to the garbage can but didn't, decide now to start tossing your garbage when you're done with it. If you didn't clear the garbage because the can was too full, go ahead and empty

LOVE YOUR CLUTTER AWAY

the can and put a clean liner/bag in it. Then, decide that part of keeping your small space clear is also emptying the garbage can when it gets full.

- If the items are recycling, make sure you have an easy way to collect the recycling. Again, if you avoided this because your recycling container was full then part of your new plan is to empty the recycling as needed.

- If the items are related to eating and leftover food then please stop now and take 3 minutes to love yourself…. Alright, ready to continue? Many clutterers also struggle with excess weight and unhealthy eating. A good part of loving your clutter away is setting up a way of living that supports and encourages yourself to live a better life. So from now on you get to enjoy eating more!

When you want to eat at your small space, first clear it off and clean it. Eating keeps you alive, so let's treat it with some respect! Bring your food to your small space, love yourself, and enjoy eating. Once you've finished, clear all your eating stuff to the kitchen, and give your small space a wipe with a clean cloth. This is now the procedure for *every* time you eat at your space. It allows you to eat consciously, with a beginning and an end to your eating time.

- If the items in your small space are illegal tenants, extra extras, or wrong room items, take each of them, and put them with the other ones you've gathered. Remember to label everything you've already sorted as you go.

- You might still have a few things to take care of. If they don't fit into the categories you already have (garbage, recycling, extras/donate, wrong room), it's time for another category – the IDK (short for I Don't Know) category. These are the things you would like to keep, but don't know where to put them. Start a bag/box for them (well labeled of course). As you continue to love your clutter away you'll create spaces for these items. When you do, be sure to collect them from the IDK box and put them in their new permanent home.

All done? Fantastic!! The truth about decluttering is that it's *not* a perfect endeavor. It takes time, effort, redos, and new thinking (and a LOT of loving yourself!). So every time you make progress – you're making progress!!

Remember **Tip #6 -** Watch out for the rest of the world. When you've cleared a small space, *you* know you've done a great thing, and *I* know you've done a great thing, but the rest of the world won't know. If you share your home with others, they probably won't be impressed with your new, clear small space. They might even be a bit of a downer. But you know it's a big deal, and you *must* congratulate yourself and keep on going!

Next, move to the entryway & path to your home, and make sure it's back to its' beautiful uncluttered state. Follow all the steps you took with your small space. Well, hopefully you won't have to do the steps for food and eating. But, if you have been eating in your hallway then I'm so pleased you cleared out this space enough to eat there! Keep on going – the rest of your house is just waiting for you to love the clutter away – and soon you'll be eating at your lovely clear table!

Ready for some fun? Once you've taken care of your entryway, review what the purpose of your entryway is:

Walk up to your house and in the door saying/singing/yelling "freedom and happiness!" Think of the feelings and love that you want coming right into your home with you.

Then walk back out of your house saying/singing/yelling "outta here!" and picture guilt, worry, and stuff that makes you sad flying right out of your home. Repeat the in and out process as many times as you want!

Finally, give that bathroom a check. Shine up the mirror if you need to, and look yourself in the eye while you say, 'I love myself'. Clean up any clutter and extras and take them to the places you've set for them.

Wow – way to go!!!! Three spaces all cleared and being used for their intended purposes!! That's fantastic – and you're fantastic!!

Now go do something fun, but when you're doing it make sure to tell yourself this is a reward for all the work you're putting into loving your clutter away. Maybe you'll read a few chapters of a book or watch a TV show. Maybe you'll go for a walk, or listen to a podcast, or go out for a coffee. Whatever you do, it's a reward for loving your clutter away – one of many to come!

SWEET DREAMS

Note: As you proceed through the book, there are some generalizations that you'll need to change to suit your situation. If you have a washer/dryer unit in your bathroom, then this is your 'laundry room'. If you don't have a home office but have a desk in your living room (or a table, or a few boxes stacked up that you put your laptop on), this is your 'home office'. If you don't have kids you don't need to go find a kids' bedroom in the neighborhood to clean. Feel free to adjust the instructions to suit your home!

Today I'll be joining you in your bedroom if you don't mind. Bedrooms are really important to our health and happiness, but they're also an amazing and powerful magnet for all kinds of things that *really* don't belong in bedrooms! I strongly believe that bedrooms should only be used for sleeping, relaxing, and sex (unless you don't have children in the house – then you're *really* going to make good use of all the new uncluttered spaces you're creating!).

Bedrooms are not for work, exercising, storage, paperwork, projects, or watching TV. I'm really firm about all of these because I *know* your sleep and relaxation will improve when you stop using your bedroom for all the other things. And when you sleep and rest better you live better. You have more energy. You make better choices. You are stronger, healthier, and happier. Good sleep and rest are absolutely critical for good health. Ideally you'll not even have your cell phone in your bedroom. But if you do, it is only to be used as an alarm, and for pleasant relaxing activities with a blue shade on at night (this helps to avoid all the harm to your sleep cycle that happens when you stare at screens instead of drifting to sleep).

If you cannot get to your side of the bed easily, start by clearing a 1 foot wide path from the door to your bed. Clear it all the way down to the floor. Sort each item into one of the following categories:

- Garbage
- Recycling
- Extras/donate
- Illegal tenants
- Wrong room
- Use it (in the bedroom) and
- IDK

Remember, whenever a bag/box gets full, take it where it belongs. The items that *do* belong in the bedroom may have to temporarily be moved out if you're short on space. Always label everything clearly so you don't have to remember what it was and where it came from. For your bedroom 'use it' items you could say: USE IT – Bedroom. Or SORTED – Bedroom.

Next, take care of your bedside table. Removing each item on top, sort it into the same categories:

- Garbage
- Recycling
- Extras/donate
- Illegal tenants
- Wrong room
- Use it (in the bedroom) and
- IDK

Wipe off the table, and the lamp if you have one. Put back the things you use *every* night. For me, this includes a lamp, my Kindle and phone with charging cords (always using blue shade at night), a small essential oils stick, a small water bottle and two small ornamental bird sculptures that I love to look at.

Once your bedside table top is set up, move to the drawer/shelf below the top. In this drawer will be things you use fairly regularly. Use the same sorting method above, and put back in the things you tend to use while in bed. Always leave some clear space. If your drawer is too full, repeat the entire process, but ask yourself if each item is actually used while you're in bed. Other items belong in a different category.

Well done! Having the path clear to your bed, and your bedside table clear are both fantastic ways of setting yourself up for better sleep. You may even find yourself looking forward to going to bed because you like what you see in your bedroom! Take 3 minutes to love yourself, and take pride in a really important job well done!

Now let's move to the top of your bed. We're working towards your bed being completely clear of clutter, and made nicely every morning. Making your bed in the morning does three things:

1. It sends a subtle message to your body that it's time to start your day
2. It creates a more peaceful look in your bedroom (whether it's full of clutter or not)
3. It creates a welcome space when bedtime arrives again.

So let's get to work clearing your bed so that you can make it! Take everything off your bed and sort it into (you guessed it) garbage, recycling, illegal tenants, use it and IDK.

Once the bed is cleared off you may want to wash the sheets. Great! Washing the sheets and making the bed will be your last love your clutter away task of the day. Far too often we start with a task like washing the sheets, forget to finish it, and then end up scrambling late at night only to end up sleeping on an unmade bed.

That's why you're going to focus on getting the sheets washed, dried and put away/put back on your bed. And then make your bed neatly. There! So nice to have a path to the bed, a cleaned up bedside table, and a nice welcoming bed. Start the habit of making the bed every day once you're up. Don't leave your bedroom in the morning unless your bed is made.

Take 3 minutes in your new bedroom space to love yourself. You're doing such a fantastic job! Thanks for sticking to it, and putting so much work into loving your clutter away! You're investing in a wonderful, peaceful home where you feel loved and happy!

If the rest of your bedroom is manageable (and you want to keep working on your bedroom), you can continue the process of loving your clutter away here. Manageable is a job that can be done within the rest of your day. (Go to chapter 14 for more details about loving your clutter away in your bedroom.) If you really had to work hard at clearing the 1 foot path, or there are still mountains of clutter to scale in your bedroom, then your job is to keep the clear spaces in your bedroom clear while you're working on the rest of the house.

KITCHEN

The kitchen is a tough area to keep clear of clutter! Either you're using it multiple times a day to prepare and cook food, or you never use it so it's been easy to pile the clutter in! If your kitchen *is* really cluttered, you'll need some small-medium sized boxes (about 6), and a good Sharpie for writing on the boxes.

Let's start with loving yourself. Take 3 minutes to breathe deeply and repeat 'I love myself' meaningfully over and over.

We'll begin loving your clutter away at the bottom – your floor. Sort through each item on your floor. Use all the standard categories (garbage, recycling, extras/donate, illegal tenants, wrong room and IDK). Instead of the 'use it' category, sort things that you think you'll keep in the kitchen into either 'Food' or 'Kitchen Items'. Use the boxes you've gathered for this, and remember to label them clearly. 'Food' is kind of self-explanatory, but please make sure you're not keeping really expired food. Try to keep the boxes so you can close and stack them when they're full. Leave them in the kitchen as much out of the way as possible.

TIP #13 – If you've had food so long that it has passed its expiry date than you've got more food than you eat in a reasonable time.

Toss it, and in the future buy smaller amounts of food that you *can* consume in a reasonable time.

TIP #14 A sale (for food or anything else) is not a bargain if it's too much to manage. Avoid buying things that will pile up in your home.

You're welcome to donate excess food to any charity that will accept it. Just remember to only donate food that hasn't expired and won't expire in the next 3 months. Remember **Tip #9** It's good to donate, but only donate good stuff!

Keep going with your floor – you are making the space to be able to get at your entire kitchen, and that's going to make everything else you do in your kitchen much easier!

Once your floor is cleared, take any full garbage, recycling, extras/donate, illegal tenants, wrong room and IDK bags/boxes to where they belong. (Remember, you may be stacking clearly labels boxes/bags of extras/donate, illegal tenants, wrong room, and IDK in a designated place in your home.) Sweep your floor, and wipe up any sticky spots with a rag/wipe.

Wow! Well done! Be very very proud of yourself for working so hard and loving your clutter away! Speaking of loving... what a great time to love yourself! Go ahead, take 3 minutes and tell your wonderful self how much you love you!

Next area to work on is the dishwasher (if you have one). Is it full of dirty dishes? Great! Go ahead and run a load. Is it full of clean dishes? Go ahead and unload it *if* you can put the dishes away in the cupboards. If you can't, just leave it for now. If it's empty you can use it to put dirty dishes in as you come across them.

Now let's clear the sink! So much fun we're having today, right?!? Again, start by taking things out one at a time, and sorting them into categories (garbage, recycling, extras/donate, illegal tenants, wrong room and IDK), and one more category – dirty dishes. If you have an empty dishwasher, start loading it. If you have a space on your counter, stack the dirty dishes there. Otherwise it's OK to stack them on the floor temporarily.

Keep going until your sink(s) is empty. Now get a rag and some cleaner and give your entire sink and faucets a good cleaning and rinse. This is really important. Kitchen sinks can be one of the germiest places in your home! If you find yourself getting sick often, try keeping your sink clean and changing your dishcloth/sponge regularly.

Remember **TIP #10** At any time if you are feeling like you just can't do anymore, remember that it's OK to stop. You're doing something that's very different than what you're used to and it can take some time to get in the groove. Always end a loving your clutter away session by taking three minutes to say 'I love myself' out loud. Then, make sure the area you were working on is left safe, take all your sorted categories to their homes, and give yourself a well-deserved break!

Next, clear 1 foot of counter space on each side of your sink. Just go one item at a time. Keep at it – you can do it! Separate into all the usual categories, and add any dirty dishes you find to your stack, wherever it is. Once each side is cleared, give it a good clean, just like you cleaned your sink.

Take a step back and have a look at what your hard work has done – pretty impressive, isn't it? Be proud of yourself!

At this point, go ahead and wash some dirty dishes that can't go in the dishwasher. Do enough to fill one counter space beside the sink with clean dishes (or dripping in a dish rack).

Now let's start making it easy to put those clean dishes away. Start with the cupboard that holds your glasses. Is there enough room in there to <u>easily</u> hold *all* of your glasses? Yes? Great, start putting your clean glasses in there. No? That's OK, we'll take care of it! Pull out any glasses you hate. Toss or donate them. This includes those ones that you'll only use if they're the last clean glass in the cupboard. You don't need to keep them anymore!

Next, throw out any broken glasses, or ones that don't look very nice. Even if this is hard, follow through. Part of the reason your kitchen gets full of stuff is that your cupboards are so full it's a pain in the butt to try and put things away. Once you make it easier to pop things in the cupboard, well, it will be easier to pop things in the cupboard! And that helps keep the kitchen tidy.

Enough room now? Great! Start putting your clean glasses away. No? OK, how many people live in your home? Double that number. Let's say there's 5 people in your family. Double that number to get 10. Now pick out your 10 most awesome glasses. Aren't they great? Toss/donate the rest, and you now have room for all your glasses! I'd bet that if there's 2 people or less living in your home that you'd like to keep more than 4 glasses. That's fine, this just gives you an idea of how much is *enough*. If each person uses 2 glasses a day, and they get washed every night after supper, then you'll always have enough glasses!

But what about when I have guests over (you ask)? Um, when was the last time you actually had so many guests over that you ran out of glasses? If this actually happened was it devastating, or just annoying? Perhaps having a kitchen full of more stuff than you can manage is devastating, and if you fix this, then being annoyed once in a while will be just fine.

You've now dealt with your glass situation! Next let's move on to plates and bowls. If you don't have space, keep the best and ditch the rest. Remember the idea of keeping twice as many of each as there are people in your home. If your space is super small, and you need to stack different sizes, that's OK. Once your cupboard has room for your plates and bowls, put the clean ones away.

Alright, now you're starting to be able to put some things away. It should feel really good! You're setting up your kitchen so it will be easy to use and keep clean – fantastic! What's the next cupboard you need to make space in? Pots and pans? Mugs? Utensils? Serving dishes? Whatever clean things are taking up room on your counter, pick that cupboard next, and make room.

Always start with getting rid of broken things, ugly things, things you've had for *ever* and never used, or things that just never worked right. And whenever you find something taking up space that you can't believe you've been keeping all this time, have a little laugh, send some loving thoughts to the person you were when you first got it, and let it go.

Kitchens can take a long time to get organized. To start, focus on the non-food cupboards you need to make space in so that things aren't on your counters. For every cupboard you create space in, stop for 3 minutes and love yourself. The work you are doing to love your clutter away is life changing for yourself and the people in your home!

TIP #15 If you share your home with others, it's inevitable that you're going to come across clutter that they created. Be very careful not to build resentment when this happens. Everyone you live with is human and needs to be loved. This is the most important. Even more important than loving your clutter away!

Once you've made room in all the cupboards you use frequently, you can start to clear more of your counters. As always, sort items into your categories (garbage, recycling, extras/donate, illegal tenants, wrong room and IDK), and enjoy putting clean dishes right into their spots in their cupboards! See how much easier that is now?! Keep up this process with each cupboard until all the non-food things in your kitchen can easily be put away.

Of course, you're going to end up with food items still on your counters (and in boxes on the floor). Maybe a lot of food items. It's this weird thing we love to do in the developed world: buy more food than we need, struggle to store it, and then end up throwing things out so we can go buy more food again. Instead, let's stop that cycle, save some money, and enjoy the food we do eat in a clean happy home.

You will have to get rid of some food to create space. Your boundaries for the amount of food you keep are the cupboards and fridge that are meant for food storage. When you can't easily put food away, you've crossed your boundaries and need to have a bit of a clear out.

Start with food that you don't like. Send it away! If it's not expired or about to expire you can donate it, but always remember **Tip #9** It's good to donate, but only donate good stuff!

Once you've gotten rid of the yucky food, move on to the food you're not likely to use in the next 2 months. You've been doing super well with loving yourself through this whole time. Now let's work on being honest with yourself. Your true self. The one under the clutter. Let that voice have a chat and pull out the things you know you're not going to use.

You know, getting rid of clutter's a bit like getting out of a really bad friendship. It may be really hard to say good bye and stick to it, but afterwards you're free – and you don't have to face their nastiness anymore because they're *gone*! Happy days!

Take 3 minutes now to love yourself. You know what to do!

Alright, back to the food. Here's how to keep on track:

- Sort through the food on your counters. Get rid of everything you don't like, and everything that should be tossed. Anything you know you won't use in 2 months (and is still good) can be donated.
- Sort through one food cupboard at a time, starting with the one you go into the most often. Repeat the process of getting rid of food so that you create space for the things you like and want to eat. Unless it's quite easy to see and touch everything in your cupboard, take each item out one at a time so you can be sure you are getting rid of all those ancient cans of food and spices way in the back of your cupboard.
- Before you start to put things back in your cupboard you need to do a bit of planning so you can put things in places where it's easy to find them. If you do have a system that works well for you, skip this step. If you don't, you'll want to make easy categories that everyone in the family can follow. Get some sticky notes, or paper and tape so you can

label each cupboard as you go. Feel free to move the notes around until you have them just the way you want them.
- When you're organizing your kitchen, try to keep things close to where you use them. For example, coffee and tea could be right beside the mugs and kettle. Here are some suggested categories. Use what works best for you. If your family really eats a lot of something you might have a cupboard just for that.

Kitchen Cupboard Storage Suggestions:

Breakfast Cupboard
-cereals, oatmeal, peanut butter, honey

Snacks Cupboard
-chips, nuts, granola bars, cookies...

School Lunch Cupboard
-all the things your kids pack in their lunch, including their lunch cases

Baking Cupboard
-ingredients for baking such as flour, sugar, baking powder, raisins...

Supper Cupboard
-things you use to make supper such as rice, pasta, pasta sauce, canned foods, mixes

Hot Drinks Shelf
-coffee, tea, hot chocolate

Generally, the cupboard you're working in will have more of one type of food. If the location is good, make that the designated cupboard for those things. Once you've cleared out everything you're not keeping, put back the things you are keeping. Try to grab everything in that category from the counters and the food that you sorted from the floor. If it all fits easily you can move to the next cupboard. If it doesn't fit, or it's so full an avalanche is imminent, go through the food again and let go of more. Remember to only keep the food you expect to use in the next 2 months.

Keep working one cupboard at a time. When you are done, the food you are keeping should be off the counters, out of the boxes/bags on the floor, and comfortably in cupboards.

The only food that stays on your counters is food you're eating nearly every day. (Well, the stuff that doesn't need refrigerating.) This is a good rule for counters in general: Only keep things out that you use nearly every day.

In my current home I have a decent amount of counter space. Here's what's on my counters: bread bin, kettle, toaster, coffee maker, sugar bowl, smoothie mixer (yep, use it nearly every day), microwave, vitamins, salt and pepper, one stand with six cooking utensils, and a spice carousel. We're a family of five and we all eat breakfast and nearly every supper at home.

Each family is different. Set up your kitchen so the things you use every day are easy to get at, and food is clearly stored in cupboards that have space to get at everything.

Remember **TIP #10** At any time if you are feeling like you just can't do anymore, remember that it's OK to stop. You're doing something that's very different than what you're used to and it can take some time to get in the groove. Always end a loving your clutter away session by taking three minutes to say 'I love myself' out loud. Then, make sure the area you were working on is left safe, take all your sorted categories to their homes, and give yourself a well-deserved break!

It's a good thing we need food to survive, or all this work in the kitchen would be pointless! As you work through your kitchen, creating space and finding homes for the things you use, you really are creating a better space to stay alive in! Good for you!

Look around at your counters. Get your sorting muscles ready, and go for it. Put one item at a time into either garbage, recycling, extras/donate, illegal tenants, wrong room or IDK. Put the things that belong in cupboards away, if you can (the cupboard has enough room). Hopefully you'll only find a few stray food items that need to go into cupboards. If you come across a surprise stash of food, just keep it in one spot until you've finished sorting everything on the counters. Remember to clearly label each bag/box that you're keeping. Take each of the sorted categories to where they belong (garbage to the trash, recycling to the bin, extras/donate with the other extras/donate, etc.)

Then you can come back to your surprise stash, eliminate everything you can, and find good homes for the rest in your food cupboards. As always, when there's not enough room, you make space by getting rid of more things.

Oh my goodness!! Now take a look at those counters will you? Fantastic job! Get a cloth and some cleaner and give them all a good wipe. Look at the things you are keeping out. Won't it make life easier now that you can get at everything? If you've made it this far and have been following the steps in the book for each room, then you're making some incredible changes that are making your life better! You're creating a safe, uncluttered, loving home!

Of course, I know that some of you are just reading the book for now. Thanks for reading this far! But wouldn't you like to feel some of this progress that I'm talking about? How about you go back to Chapter 5 – Warming Up and get your small space cleared? You *can* do it! Go ahead, I'll be right here with you cheering you on!

If you've just finished wiping off those gorgeous cleared counters, and you haven't taken a break recently, please stop and take a break. Eat something from your lovely cupboards, go for a walk, even watch a show. In this time, take 3 minutes to love yourself. When you've taken a break, come on back to the kitchen.

Ready for what's next? You may have figured it out already – the fridge (perhaps some more scary music is in order!). I'll be honest here, the fridge is one of my least favorite places to organize. It's cold in there! But what I *do* like is being able to easily take what I need in and out of the fridge without having to shove, wiggle, stack or balance. So let's get the fridge taken care of!

Fortunately, you have less categories to sort this time! Get a really good strong double/triple bag for garbage. Yeah, that's about it! Of course, there will be jars that you can recycle. But the stuff in your fridge is either good quality food you'll be eating soon, or it's garbage.

Start at the top shelf of the door of the fridge. Take everything out. Wipe any sticky spots/spills. Check expiry dates and only keep good food. If there are jars/containers that need to be emptied, put them on your (clear and clean!) counter beside the (clear and clean!) sink. Then move on to the next shelf down and do the same thing.

Watch out for salad dressings. Many people tend to stock way too many in their fridge, and then leave them for eternity. But salad dressings expire, and expired salad dressing doesn't exactly improve the health of your salad! Get rid of all but three, and keep to no more than three.

Once you've worked your way down each shelf in the door, move to the top shelf of the fridge. Again, take everything out. Wipe down spills/stickiness. Get rid of all old/expired/gross food. Put the keepers back. Move to the next shelf. When you get down to the fruit and veggie drawers, take them out completely. Then take all the food out of the drawer. Get rid of everything you won't eat in the next week. Wash the drawers in your (clean and clear!) sink before drying them, then putting them back in the fridge with only the fresh, tasty food you're going to eat this week back in them.

Last loving your clutter away stop in the kitchen! The freezer portion of your fridge. Again, start with the door. Take everything out. Toss everything old, gross, or unidentifiable into a triple bag. Toss everything you won't eat in the next 3 months. Put the food you'll actually eat back on the shelves.

Move to the main part of the freezer, and work down each shelf one at a time. Take everything out. Toss everything old, gross, or unidentifiable into a triple bag. Toss everything you won't eat in the next 3 months. Replace the food you'll actually eat. (sound familiar?)

One more thing about the freezer.... Are you using it to store batteries, photo film, or other non-food items? That's OK, but follow these rules:

- Food comes first. If the objects are making it difficult to get your food in, you need to keep less non-food items in the fridge.
- Only keep what you use. If you've had batteries or film sitting in your freezer for years, then you're wasting electricity freezing things you'll likely never use. Recycle the batteries and toss the film.

When you've finished sorting your fridge and freezer, take care of anything you've put on the counter. Clean things out, recycle what you can, and throw out the garbage. When you're done, the kitchen will look marvelous – clean and clear counters, clean and clear sink, and clear floor that's safe to walk around on! You've done a wonderful job!

Since the kitchen often sees the most activity in the house, it can be hard to keep tidy. Here are some great kitchen rules you can follow:

1. Have a firm schedule for the dishwasher. Run it every night if you share your home with others, or set days if there's one or two people in the home (such as every Monday, Wednesday and Friday). Put a reminder in your phone and in your kitchen about what days are dishwasher days.
2. Have a firm schedule for unloading the dishwasher. If you run it every night, then unload it every morning. Make sure it's run after a meal, and unloaded before the next meal so there's no reason to pile dirty dishes on the counter.

*Remember, you've set up your cupboards to have room for all your dishes, so unloading the dishwasher will be a breeze.

*Get the family involved! Even a 3 year old can put in a dishwasher tab and press start, and unload their plastic dishes and cups.

> 3. NEVER buy groceries unless you've checked your fridge, cleaned out the old food, and written a list. Always make your grocery list in the kitchen where you can check to see what items you already have.

(Clutterers often get in the habit of buying things they've run out of in the past – repeatedly. Making a thoughtful list will stop you from having 8 bottles of ketchup in the cupboard and buying 2 more on your next grocery trip.)

> 4. Every night after supper, clean off the table, the counters and the stove. Put all dirty dishes in the dishwasher (and remember to start it!), wash everything that needs hand washing, and rinse out the sink. I *know* that after a long day the last thing you want to do is tidy the kitchen. But I *also* know that coming into a clean kitchen in the morning is the nicest way to start your day and it's worth it!

You've done it! You've cleared and cleaned your kitchen! Three hundred cheers for you! Really let yourself feel how amazing you are, and how proud you are of this really tough job that you just managed! Take 3 minutes now and repeat 'I love myself' in your wonderful kitchen.

LAUNDRY ROOM

Next to cooking, laundry is generally the most time consuming chore in the home. For many clutterers, laundry is much harder because their laundry area is difficult to access, there's nowhere to sort dirty clothes and fold clean clothes, and it's difficult to get to closets and dressers to put clean clothes away.

So when you love away your clutter in the laundry room, you are making a job you have to do every week *much* easier. Let's get started.

First stop is the floor. Of course you'll be sorting each item into garbage, recycling, extras/donate, illegal tenants, wrong room or IDK. But you'll also have laundry to sort. If you do have access to some empty laundry baskets, get those out to sort into. Otherwise you can use some bags/boxes, but be sure to label them with big clear labels.

The best way to get on top of your laundry (aside from climbing it) is to keep your system as simple as possible. I recommend two categories: white laundry, and non-white laundry. I'm not kidding! This is a system the whole family can follow, and it works. Since most detergents now work in cold water, if you wash all your laundry in cold then even the delicates can be sorted into one of the two categories.

It's going to take a while to get through all the laundry, but it's going to feel soooo good when you do! When you are sorting things on the floor, make a path to the washing machine first. Then, let's play choose your story here:

Option A: If your washing machine is full, go to Option B. If it is empty, do a little happy dance! When you have gathered a load of dirty laundry, put it right in the washer and start the load. Make sure the buzzer is on to tell you when it's finished, or set a reminder on your phone for when to check on the finished load. Then go to Option F.

Option B: If the washing machine has a load of damp clothes in it and they've been there for a day or more, run the load again. Once you've started the load, make sure the buzzer is on to tell you when it's finished, or set a reminder on your phone for when to check on the finished load. Then go to Option F.

Option C: If the washing machine has a load of damp clothes in it and they're ready to go in the dryer, then go to Option D.

Option D: Make a path to the dryer. (When you make a path, do it by sorting each item as you go. Don't just throw everything out of the way. That way you're only sorting through things once.) When you get to the dryer, if it's empty go to Option E. If it's not empty, go to Option F.

Isn't this fun?

Option E: Do a little happy dance, and move the load from the washer to the dryer and turn on the dryer. Make sure the buzzer is on to tell you when it's finished, or set a reminder on your phone for when to check on the finished load. Proceed to Option F.

Option F: Continue to clear the floor one item at a time. When the floor is clear, proceed to Option G.

Option G: If you don't have a counter for folding laundry in the laundry area, go to option H. If you do have a counter, start to clear it off by sorting each item into garbage, recycling, extras/donate, illegal tenants, wrong room or IDK, plus of course your white and not-white dirty laundry. If you have clean laundry on the counter, set it to the side in a bag/basket. When the counter is clear (YAY! Well done!) wipe it clean. This is now your space for folding clean laundry! Now move to Option I.

Option H: Take your clean laundry to your kitchen counter for folding. Once you've cleared other areas of your home (such as your table) there may be a better place. For now the kitchen counter is your space for folding clean laundry. Go to Option I.

Option I: Fold all of your clean laundry, putting it into piles according to how you put it away. (For example, if you separate long sleeve and short sleeve t-shirts then have two piles. If you keep all your t-shirts together then put them all in one pile when they're folded). Go to Option J.

Option J: Check and see if it's time to change your laundry over, if it is, transfer your laundry, and fold all clean, dry laundry. Go to Option K.

Option K: Are there any other areas in your laundry room that have clutter (such as cupboards and shelves)? If not, go to Option L. If yes, tackle each space, on at a time. Sort into all your laundry room categories: garbage, recycling, extras/donate, illegal tenants, wrong room, IDK, white laundry and non-white laundry. Go to Option L.

Option L: If you can switch over your laundry do it now. Fold all clean dry laundry. Then put all the sorted items in their homes, and take the clean laundry to wherever it goes. If you can't get the clean laundry all the way to its home (For example, if your linen closet is too full for more linens, or you can't get to your dresser), put it in a clean bag labelled 'Clean _____ to go in the _____'(fill in the blanks appropriately) and put it as close as possible. Go to Option M.

Option M: Clean the laundry room. Wipe down the counter and the washer and dryer, and vacuum and then wash the floor. When you think about it, this area is best kept clean – it's what produces all your clean laundry! Now you don't have to worry when clean clothes fall on the floor – just pick them up because they're still clean! Now, let's make a plan for keeping on top of the laundry.

There are two excellent methods for handling laundry. Choose the one that works for you and stick to it. At first, it may be hard to remember that you have a laundry plan, so write it down where you'll see it, and put a reminder in your phone for every laundry day.

Option 1 – Once a Week Laundry

This is the one I use because I want 6 days a week when I *don't* have to think about laundry. Choose a day of the week when you'll be home for the day. First thing in the morning, gather enough laundry for the first load, and go start the load. (by first thing I mean *first* thing unless you only have a load or two in total to do) Then gather the rest of the laundry, take it to the laundry room, and sort it so it's ready to be washed. Set a timer so you'll remember to switch over the laundry as soon as it's done washing. Every time a load is dry, full the entire load right away. When the last load is done and folded, take all clean laundry back to where it belongs. The job isn't done until the laundry is all back where it belongs. Bonus points if you can get all the ironing done the same day too! (Which I manage to do about one week out of every two…)

Option 2 – Every Day Laundry

This is a great option for people who don't want the laundry to pile up much. It will work best if you keep all dirty laundry right in the laundry room so you're not traipsing through the house looking for dirty laundry every morning. With this method, you start a load of laundry as soon as you get up. If you have to go to work, make sure you get up early enough to transfer the load to the dryer before you leave. If you'll be at home set a time so you remember to transfer the laundry to the dryer, and then fold it right away when it's dry. When the load is folded, take all the clean laundry back to where it belongs. The job isn't done until the laundry is all back where it belongs.

If you have no idea which one to choose, pick one, try it for a few weeks, and then try the other one for a few weeks. The best choice for you is the one where you are most likely to finish the job every time.

Here's some laundry tips:

- Get all kids 12 and up to do their own laundry. By this age they generate enough dirty clothes to do a load of whites and non-whites every week. Take the time to teach them how to use the machines. (You can put a 'how to' sheet on the wall if they have trouble remembering.) At first you may have to keep at them to start, transfer, fold, and put away their laundry. But they *can* do it!

This is excellent for the kids on so many levels. They start to understand that clean clothes take time and effort (instead of getting mad at you for not having their laundry done!) Your girls will start to realize that throwing clean clothes in the laundry means more work for them. And your kids will all develop an essential life skill! It also makes your laundry pile smaller and easier to use.

- Kids under 12 can help by putting their own laundry away, and even doing some folding.
- Put a hook up in the laundry room that can hold a bunch of hangers. Hang everything that needs ironing up on a hanger as soon as the dryer stops – you'll have less wrinkles to deal with.

Oh my goodness! Was that a big job? Congratulations! You've just done another huge thing that will make your life easier and better every week! Go take the rest of the day off – you deserve it!!

YOUR VEHICLE

By now you may be starting to need to make some trips to the thrift store/dump/recycling – if you haven't already. That's excellent news, because it shows that you're taking real action to love your clutter away!

Let's make those trips nicer by loving the clutter away in your vehicle. Before you head over to it, get a bag(s) for garbage, a bag for recycling (make this a big bag if there's lots of empty bottles in your vehicle), a box labelled 'Wrong Room – Car', a box labelled 'Donate', a bag for 'Use it' that will hold the items that belong in the car and a box labelled IDK. Remember, IDK is the category for anything you have no idea what to do with, or you can't decide what to do with it.

Start at the driver's side. Working your way from the dashboard down to the floor, take each thing out one at a time and sort it into the right category. When you've finished, do the same on the front passenger side, then the glove box, and then work your way through to the very back. The last place to sort out will be the trunk, if you have one.

When you're finished sorting, take a look at your 'Use it' items. Can you easily and safely store them in your vehicle without them rolling around, or taking up much space? If not, give them another sort before putting them away into secure places in your car. Take all the sorted items to their homes, *unless* you had a vehicle full of items you planned to donate. If this is the case, put everything else away, and then get in the car and go donating!

Remember **TIP #1** If you are donating things at a thrift store or charity shop *do not* go in and look around. *Do not* put a single thing back in your care. Make this a rule that you always follow.

On your way back from donating (or after you've put everything away), take your car for a wash and vacuum. Ahhhhh…..Isn't it so much nicer to be able to just slip into the driver's seat without moving anything, and to drive in a clean and clear vehicle? So now you can keep it that way with the following rules:

- As much as possible, avoid eating in the car. If you do eat in the car, remove all trash the first time you stop after eating. Be like one of those strange picky people that puts every scrap of garbage in the can right after they use it.
- Speaking of garbage, place some sort of container/bag in the vehicle to hold garbage. Make sure you can reach it from the driver's seat easily. If you drive kids around, make sure there's one that they can reach too. Empty it regularly.
- Only put things you need to take somewhere (donations, recycling, store returns) into the car on the day you will be taking them. If you tend to forget about stopping, write it on a sticky note and put it on your (clean!) dash as a reminder. Your car is not a storage unit. As you clear your home, you will have room to keep the things you need in your home. The rest is clutter, and it's a great day to love your clutter away!

Finish your fantastic job on your vehicle with 3 minutes of saying 'I love myself' out loud.

THE FRONT CLOSET AND ENTRYWAY

Hello again!

Guess what? You've got a clean vehicle ready to take your clutter away! Now let's move back inside – just inside to your front closet and entryway. But before we go further, let's think about what your entry is for (bear with me here!). Really, it's for coming and going, right? Not for stopping and dropping... In plain terms, the entryway cannot be used for storage.

As you love the clutter away in the rest of your home, it will be much easier to put things away. But you're still going to have to put them away. Which means not putting them down when you come in the door and leaving them there. Or shoving them in the closet.

Remember the sayings you practiced way at the beginning of the book when you cleared a pathway into your home? Go ahead and do it again for fun:

Walk up to your house and in the door saying/singing/yelling "freedom and happiness!" Think of the feelings and love that you want coming right into your home with you. Then walk back out of your house saying/singing/yelling "outta here!" and picture guilt, worry, and stuff that makes you sad flying right out of your home. Repeat the in and out process as many times as you want!

Wasn't that fun?! Let's create a really great system for *all* of your entryway areas now, so you can keep on enjoying more and more freedom and happiness in your home.

Since your entryway is the main way in and out of your home, you want to keep it as clear and welcoming as possible. Start with the standard sorting, one item at a time until you've cleared the whole area from wall to wall. The categories are garbage, recycling, extras/donate, illegal tenants, use it, wrong room and IDK.

Under your 'use it' category it's reasonable to include the following (if you have space):

- Two jackets/coats per family member (the most frequently used ones)
- Two pairs of shoes/boots per family member (again, the most frequently used ones)
- Umbrellas if it rains at least once a week
- Purses
- School bags if there's room.

All other items can be returned to the owner's bedroom. So that may mean you're making some trips to people's bedrooms this time. Normally you could put things into 'Wrong room' but since they may be needed just drop them off in bedrooms instead.

You may have noticed throughout the whole book that I have not made one single suggestion to go out and buy anything. But that's about to change! Because one of the most important things to have in your entryway is hooks for coats and shelves for shoes. Even if you have a coat closet for hanging coats (more on that soon), if you have ever just dropped your coat on the floor when you came in the door than a hook is the right solution for you!

Hooks are pretty much universally useful when put at the right height. Everyone from toddlers to teenagers to spouses can toss their coat on a hook when they come in the door. *If* there is a vacant hook, and *if* it's easy for them to get to. A hook can often do double duty, hanging a purse and a coat, or a backpack and a coat. Hooks are awesome!

Shoe shelves are not quite as awesome, but they are super handy for increasing the storage ability of your entryway. If you don't have something already, make sure you get something that won't take up much space, is easy to put shoes on and off of, and is easy to clean.

Of course, hooks and shelves are no good if you don't use them, so make sure you get a great return from your purchases and keep them in good use! If they allow you to keep more shoes and coats in the entryway, that's fine. Within reason.

In our family of 5, each person has 3 shoe cubbies for their shoes. They're welcome to keep more than 3 pairs of shoes there as long as they fit into the 3 cubbies. It's a pretty good number, since it allows for school shoes, runners, soccer/dance shoes and a pair of slippers shoved in.

OK, back to the wonderful business of loving your clutter away. You've clear the entire space in your entryway from wall to wall. You've decided which coats, shoes, and bags are used often enough to be allowed the honor of staying here. If things are getting crowded, take all your sorted items to their homes.

Next is the coat closet. (If you don't have one, skip on by this section.) Boy oh boy, do people ever store the most interesting things in their front closets! Starting with the hanging items, take each thing out, and sort it into a category. Since you're fortunate enough to have a coat closet, you can certainly store a few more coats in here. Maybe even the seasonal ones you're not using right now (like winter coats, if it's summer out). But only if there's room to <u>easily</u> take them in and out. No shoving and squeezing allowed.

Once you've sorted the hanging items, and you've put the ones you want to keep in the closet on your 'Use it' pile, move to the top of the closet. Be careful, and watch out for potential avalanches as you take each item out and sort it into its category.

You can keep 'Use it' items to fill up to half this shelf – keep the other half empty.

Now move down to the bottom of the closet and do the same thing. I hope you have a good laugh when you find strange and unusual things down there! In some houses this is the best place to store things like the vacuum cleaner and tall boots. That's OK, as long as there's room. You also need to leave a 1 foot wide space clear at here. Go ahead and return your 'Use it' items to the closet. If it's hard to fit things in still, take another sort. Remember to get rid of things that are broken, worn out, don't work well, or are rarely used.

The two spaces in your closet have special purposes that should make your life easier. On the shelf the space is for things that need to make a special journey. This is where the clothes that your son's absent-minded friend forgets at your house get put to be returned to him. And where the book you borrowed from your friend goes to be returned. And where your daughter's birthday gift for her friend's party goes so you can grab it on the way out the door this Saturday. Or whatever things you will be carrying out will go.

The space at the bottom of the closet is for your Donate Bag. This is an essential item for every home! Even people with no clutter come across things they need to donate! Have this bag accessible at the front door, and make sure the whole family knows about it. Whenever you have something to donate, pop it in the bag. When the bag is full, donate it, and put another empty bag in its place. You will be amazed at how much stuff you'll find to donate after you've loved your clutter away! This system makes it so easy to keep up the good work.

If there are any other areas in your entryway, please go ahead and love the clutter away in each of them. Take one item at a time, and sort it into garbage, recycling, extras/donate, illegal tenants, use it, wrong room or IDK. Then take each category to where it belongs and enjoy your fabulous entryway!!

Of course, this area needs to be maintained, and that may take some practice. Be patient with everyone (including yourself), but consistently expect everyone to use the hooks and shoe shelves, and *not* drop and leave things here.

THE MASTER BEDROOM

By now the action of meaningfully loving yourself is (hopefully) a good part of your life every day. Which is part of the reason I've left the rest of the master bedroom alone until now. When I first started working with clutterers I always wanted them to declutter their master bedroom first, so that they could start sleeping better right away, and get in the practice of taking care of themselves better – or so I thought!

But when you try to declutter your bedroom before you're really loving yourself, it's really hard to complete and even harder to maintain. Many clutterers are used to putting their own needs last, so they tend to find it easier to declutter spaces where others will benefit first. Which you have definitely done! Now it's time for you.

Take 3 minutes now to sit on your bed and say 'I love myself' over and over. Imagine that love filling you up, and floating in the air around you and on your bed. Picture yourself resting in your bedroom and feeling loved.

Like I said before, bedrooms should only be used for sleeping, resting, and sex. Of course, resting can mean lots of different things (curling up in a cozy bed with a delicious book comes to mind right away!) So keep things in your bedroom that are restful to you. Things that are *not* restful cannot live here anymore.

Let's start with the first areas you worked on in here: a path to the bed, your bedside table, and the top of your bed. Clear all clutter from these three spaces using your categories - garbage, recycling, extras/donate, illegal tenants, use it, wrong room and IDK. Remember to put things into clearly labelled bags. Clean clothes can go in a separated 'Use it' bag/box, and add a category for dirty clothes. If you have a clothes hamper/basket available use this for your dirty clothes.

When you come across things that aren't restful, make sure they are in one of the categories that will be leaving your room. After you've cleared these three spaces, make your bed if it's not made already.

Go back to the door into your bedroom, and start to clear your floor one item at a time, moving in a counter clockwise direction. Remember that anything that doesn't make you feel restful doesn't belong in the bedroom. As you work your way through your room, keep loving yourself. Whenever a bag/box gets full from sorting, take it to its home and get another empty one. Remember **TIP #5** When you are returning an item to its home (or closer to its home if you can't get all the way there) do not stop, do not pass go, but go straight back to where you were working.

When you've finished the floor, stop and give yourself a break. Grab a bit to eat, so some stretches, maybe get some fresh air. Reminder yourself that you love you, and that you're doing a fantastic job of loving your clutter away!

Back in your bedroom, it's time to make it easy to put your clothes away. (You may be noticing something at this point – loving your clutter away is a lot about making things easier for yourself. While the actual letting go of things can be hard, the result is geared towards making everything in your life easier. Loving your clutter away is the best way to have less work in your house, giving you time for more fun!)

So, to the closet(s)! The sorting here gets done a bit differently. You will likely still find 'Wrong room', 'Illegal tenants', and even some garbage, so keep those categories going. But when it comes to your clothes we do things a bit differently. Each item gets an initial sort into 'Ah' (you like it!), 'Ugh' (you don't like it!), and IDK (you have no idea). Keep to those three short words with every item.

If your closet is exploding with clothes, and you find yourself putting everything into 'Ah', stop for a minute. What do clothes mean to you? Have they been a way of disguising how you feel about yourself? Because now that you're loving yourself, you don't need to hide behind clothes anymore. You *know* you're a pretty great person! And its time to wear the things that really reflect who you are. Try again with the sorting and love yourself as you pick the best clothes for the real you, and 'Ugh' the rest.

If your closet is exploding with clothes because of a past where you didn't have many clothes, then this is another time to stop for a minute. Think back to the person you were when you didn't have very much (or you didn't have any nice things). Love that person. Imagine you're going back in time, and give the old you with the ugly clothes a long hug. Tell that person that you were that you love them. And then let them go. Now that you love yourself, it's love that fills you up from the inside – not the clothes that you put on the surface.

Of course you can still have lots of fun with clothes, and enjoy wearing nice things. But you no longer need to keep clothes to try and feel loved. You are loved. Nice clothes are just a bonus. Go back to your sorting while remembering that you are loved. You may begin to remember feelings you had when you bought different clothes. A lot of the time the clothes were bought when you were feeling down. Now it's not the clothes that make you feel loved – it's *you* that makes you feel loved. So stick to the 'Ah' clothes and ditch the rest!

Once you've cleared out your entire closet (Yay! Well done!), you get to put things back. Hang things up in categories so it's easier (there's that word again!) to find things from now on. Good categories are: Long sleeve tops, short sleeve tops, skirts, pants, dresses/suits and coats. Make sure you have a tiny bit of room between each item, and at least 10% of your hanging space is still empty. If this isn't the case, have another sort.

When you've emptied out your closet, and put the clothes back in, and left some hanging space, give yourself a big high five!! Way to go!! Take a break, get a snack...(you know the drill) and love yourself for 3 minutes before coming back to your closet.

You'll still have things to go back in your closet. Try to only put things back in related to you and your clothes. If you can find a different place in your home for wrapping paper and gift bags and suitcases and sports gear and whatever else isn't really about clothes, then please do. It can all be 'Wrong Room' for now. The remaining shoes, bags, and hats can go back in within the space limits of your closet. If the things can't fit in, then it's time for another sort. Only keep the very best things you really like to wear. If you've got a name brand purse that's *really* expensive (or perhaps a suit if you're a gentleman) but you've never used/worn it, let it go.

Tip #16 Your house isn't a storage unit. No matter how expensive something was, if it's not usable and wonderful *to you* it needs to go. If your first reason for keeping something is how much it cost, that's a sign that it's <u>not</u> something you need to keep.

Take any full bags/boxes to their homes, and then step back and enjoy your brand new, accessible and easy-to-use closet! Fantastic!

Alright, let's move to your dresser. I do recommend you only have one dresser per person. Even less will work. More dressers just means more buried clothes that you spend money on and don't wear.

Start at the top of the dresser. Sort each item into garbage, recycling, extras/donate, illegal tenants, use it, wrong room and IDK. If you come across anything that belongs in your closet, you can dance over and put it there – that's why you left some room in it. Separate 'Use its' that you want on your dresser from 'Use its' that belong elsewhere in your bedroom. Once the top is cleared wipe it clean. If there's a mirror/hutch as part of the dresser, clear it off as well, and give it all a nice polish.

Replace the 'Use its' that you want on your dresser, making sure that they use less than half of the surface. You can put a few beautiful things that make you happy there – but only a few. You can also leave things on your dresser that you use nearly every day. The rest will be 'Use its' for other places.

Next get some sticky notes and a marker, and label each drawer with what you plan to keep there. Since I was a child I've had the same system for drawers: from top to bottom they hold underclothes and socks, shirts, pants, sweaters, pyjamas. It makes it easy to find things, easy to put things away, and easy to move houses (well, easier at least). With the advent of great closet organizers some people are even doing away with their dresser.

I've found that shelves are a great solution for clutterers. It's just easier to put things _on_ something rather than _in_ something (this can work well for teens too). The key is to have the shelves somewhere they can be hidden (like in a closet), and to keep the stacks of clothes on the shelves a manageable height and easy to get at.

OK, so back to the dressers. Once you've labelled them, start with the top drawer. Take everything out. Sort into the usual categories, and then put the 'Use it' items that fit the label on the drawer back in. Continue working your way through each drawer. At any point, if the drawer gets too full to easily put clothes in and take them out, then have another sort so you're only keeping the nicest clothes that you really like to wear. (Don't bother keeping nice clothes that will only look good on someone else!)

Remember **Tip #16** Your house isn't a storage unit. No matter how expensive something was, if it's not usable and wonderful _to you_ it needs to go. If your first reason for keeping something is how much it cost, that's a sign that it's not something you need to keep.

How's your room looking? Do you still have places that need the clutter loved away? First, take 3 minutes to love yourself. Then move to the place closest to your dresser. Follow the steps for sorting, and putting back 'Use its' without filling the space. Once you're done, move to place closest, and keep going!

This is really exciting! Do you know how many people dream of getting the clutter out of their bedrooms but never do? You're not just a dreamer – you're a doer! And just think of all the sweet dreams you'll have in your wonderful, peaceful bedroom!

Remember, every morning when you're up, make your bed. It doesn't have to be perfect, or have a gazillion decorative pillows arranged across it (who has time for that?!?), just made.

THE DINING ROOM

The dining room is a really important room for establishing quality family time, good eating habits, and wonderful memories. The thing is, it's easy to let the dining room fill up with stuff. You can always eat at the couch, or the counter, or in your room. And if your house is cluttered you won't want to have guests over for a meal.

Even if your main table isn't in its own room, treat it and the space around it like the dining room. Start with the floor. Beginning closest to the entry/door, sort through each item one at a time. Use your categories of garbage, recycling, extras/donate, illegal tenants, use it, wrong room and IDK.

The truth is that the dining room should have little in it besides a table and chairs, and maybe a buffet/hutch that holds some dishes and dishware. When this is the case, it makes a lovely, relaxing place to eat a meal. If you live alone, creating a less cluttered dining space and then using it regularly will be good for you. It's a nice treat to eat at the couch, but please don't make it a habit. Food is too important to be thoughtlessly consumed without paying attention to where you're eating.

OK, so back to the floors. You'll probably find a lot of 'Wrong room' in here, since it's pretty common to turn the dining area into a storage room. As you love the clutter away throughout your house it will be easier to put things away in the room they belong in, and stop using the dining area for all those things. Once the spaces you have in your rooms have reached their boundaries (ie. bookshelves are full, closets are full), then it's time to pare down your things some more.

When you've cleared the floor, stop and celebrate! And be sure to take 3 minutes (or more) to breathe deeply and repeat 'I love myself' out loud. Move to the surface of the table next.

Remember the tip for paperwork: **TIP #3** When you come across paperwork, your main task is to separate the urgent from the mountain(s). Urgent means you must deal with it or face serious consequences. Bills are urgent. Coupons are not urgent. Legal summons are urgent. Newsletters are not urgent. Place the urgent items in a visible container that will ONLY hold urgent paperwork. Place the rest of the paperwork in a box labelled 'papers' or something similar that makes sense to you.

When the surface of the table is clear, give it a polish and then enjoy the view! Move to the chairs first, clearing and sorting the things off one chair at a time until they're all clear. If you couldn't get to some of the spaces on the floor, you should be able to now. So again, sort through each item one at a time, putting each into the right category.

If you have a bag/box full of sorted items, go ahead and take it to its spot. Remember **TIP #5** When you are returning an item to its home (or closer to its home if you can't get all the way there) do not stop, do not pass go, but go straight back to where you were working. By now you'll be building up a decent pile of paperwork, a pile of Wrong room, and a pile of IDK.

Once you have some donations together, go ahead and take them in, and always follow **TIP #1** If you are donating things at a thrift store or charity shop *do not* go in and look around. *Do not* put a single thing back in your care. Make this a rule that you always follow.

Next, if you have anything else in your dining room, like a hutch/buffet, sort through it now. Starting from the top and working your way down, take each item, put it into garbage, recycling, extras/donate, illegal tenants, use it, wrong room or IDK. Give it a nice wipe with a cloth, and then put the items back on/in it that you want there. If it doesn't all easily fit with some room to space then sort it all again, looking for the things you can move out of your home. If you're having trouble with this, pick your absolute favorite things, put them in/on your buffet, and move the rest into an IDK box.

It's nice to have *some* things in your dining room that bring back good memories, or make you smile. Eating while you're happy is good for your soul and your body, so have some smile-inducing things in your dining room to enjoy while you eat.

Is there any other area in your dining room that needs clutter loved away? Continue with the process until everything has been sorted into categories, the categories that don't belong in the dining room have been put where they go, and the things that are staying in the dining room are put neatly in their homes or on display to enjoy.

Done! Actually, that's well done! Congratulations on this fantastic dining room! May it frequently be used to enjoy good food with the people you love!

THE LIVING ROOM

We've made it to the living room. What do you do in here? Do you watch TV, or read? Do your kids play in here? Practice piano? Eat? Let's set up the living room so that the things you do in here can be done comfortably, with space to move around, and places to put away the things you use. Except for the eating. Now that there's a lovely clear table in the dining area, eat your meals there (although there will likely still be some eating in the living room, try to eat your meals in the dining room only.

The most important thing here? Take 3 minutes to love yourself. Be meaningful each time you say 'I love myself'. Remind yourself of all the places in your home you've cleared, and name any positive feelings you're experiencing as a result. You may be feeling proud, loved, impressed, hopeful...whatever the feelings are, just be conscious of them.

As always, let's start by making a path if the floor is covered. The path should be about a foot wide from the entrance to the couch. Sort through each item one at a time, putting the into garbage, recycling, extras/donate, illegal tenants, use it, wrong room and IDK.

Once this path is clear, start working around the room in a clockwise (or counter clockwise if you're feeling a bit wild) direction, starting from your path and continuing to make it wider as you work your way around the room.

Pay a bit of attention to the items that don't belong. How did they get there and how can you keep them out? If you have lots of garbage, maybe a small garbage can in the livingroom would be helpful. If you found lots of food, or the remnants of food then eating in the dining room will decrease this. If you find things that were left here because you didn't have room somewhere else for them, think about where their new home can be, and how you can make it easier to put things away from now on.

Once the floor is completely clear you should probably do a happy dance around the room. Doesn't it feel nice not to step on things or bump into things?! Way to go!!

Now let's get the couch/sofas/seating things cleared. Start closest to the door, working your way across each couch, sorting every item and putting them into garbage, recycling, extras/donate, illegal tenants, use it, wrong room and IDK.

Once this is done, go back and take the cushions of the first couch. Hopefully you'll find lots of money! Sort everything you find and add a category for your new found wealth. Give a careful feel into the black holes along the edges for extra money and the missing remote controls. Fun, right! Replace the cushions and move to the next sofa/chair. Repeat until you've found all of your lost fortune.

If you've found some money you may need to do another happy dance. While you're dancing take 3 minutes to say (shout?) out loud 'I love myself' over and over.

Let's take care of the coffee table and end tables next. It's the same process as before. Start with the table closest to the door. Clear off each item, sorting into garbage, recycling, extras/donate, illegal tenants, use it, wrong room and IDK. And add one more category – magazines! When you've sorted everything on it, give it a wipe, and put back only the things you use nearly every day, and a few decorative items.

Move to the next table and repeat until every coffee table/side table/end table is clean and shiny and displaying some lovely treasure that makes you smile. Now, are you ready for something a little different? Usually your sorted categories are taken to their temporary homes (well, except for garbage, recycling and donations), but let's take a look at those magazines for a minute.

Magazines can be a clutterer's kryptonite. They come to your house all shiny and new, giving you pictures of the perfect life that can be yours, all just for reading a magazine. Quite the trap, isn't it? Because all those lovely pictures are in magazines that are cluttering up your house. Don't get me wrong, I love looking at those pictures too! But you have to be careful not to get into the trap of thinking you need the magazines to have a perfect life. Life will never be perfect, and magazines will never clean your house for you.

If you get subscriptions, cancel them except for your favorite magazine (this is the one you actually read when it comes). You can always start up a subscription later, but signing up to have clutter delivered to your door every month is not a good thing for you right now. It's pretty easy to cancel. First, find the subscriptions number inside the magazine. It should be on the page with all the boring small print. Next, look at the mailing label on the magazine. It has the information on it that they'll ask you for when you call and cancel. Go ahead and give them a call and request to cancel your subscription immediately. Do NOT let them con you into extending it, even if they offer you a deal! You need this break in order to get in front of your clutter. Repeat for the other magazines you need to cancel.

Great! That's one step that will really help keep clutter away! Now you've got to take a look at the magazines that have already made it into your living room. I *know* you want to read them. I *know* there's this great article that feels really important to you. And I know that tantalizing recipe is just waiting to be clipped out and saved in some mountainous pile of clippings.

But more than all that, I *know* that you are a wonderful person without the magazines. Having them doesn't make you any better than you already are (you're awesome!), and getting rid of them doesn't make you any worse of a person. So, take a deep breath, say 'I love myself' a few times, and let's sort the magazines. Keep the current editions, and put the rest in a bag/box. You can leave the current editions on your coffee table.

The rest of the magazines can be recycled, or donated. Most thrift stores take magazines, but you can also drop off relatively current magazines at any waiting room in your area. (Ask the receptionist first of course.)

Whenever you get a new edition, replace the previous one with the new one, and get rid of the old one. Especially if you haven't read it! Because if you're not reading it every month, what's the point of paying to have it jump into your house on a regular basis? I know this is hard for some people. We just want more information than we actually take time to consume. So do your best to enjoy the few magazines that you read, and stop the rest from coming (and send those old ones to another home!)

Phew! There's a lot of changes happening as you love your clutter away. It's really fantastic that you're sticking to it! Well done you!!

I think it's time to tackle the area around the TV. You know, just 8 years ago it was a big deal that DVDs were such a thing. They were SO much smaller than VHS' and way easier to store! Now, DVDs are becoming way less of a thing as we access more of our entertainment digitally. I'm all for this, since it *can* make this area in your living room less cluttered. The problem comes when you don't get rid of your old media as you add new media. The solution (or part of it) is that a lot of old stuff can be accessed digitally right now if you really need to re-watch a beloved movie in the future.

Let's start with VHS tapes. Start sorting them, and putting as many as you can into the garbage. Don't bother keeping the old movies your kids used to love when they were little. They can already find them online whenever they want. If you find any home movies in there that you want to keep, put them into the 'Wrong room' category. Then later you can find out where to send them to get them made into digital files.

Once the VHS tapes are gone, move on to the DVDs. Really consider only keeping your best dozen or so. The rest can be donated to charity. There's so much excellent content available online, on demand, and digitally now that you really can downsize your physical collection without downsizing your access to lots of great movies!

Sort through everything else in, around, and on your TV. Remember those categories - garbage, recycling, extras/donate, illegal tenants, use it, wrong room and IDK.

If you've got young kids, you've probably got a lot of toys kicking around your living room. Choose a small basket/decorative box to hold some toys, and put the rest into 'Wrong room' or 'Donate'. They'll get used to being surrounded by less, and have more fun playing when they have less choice about *what* to play with, and less to clean up when they're done.

How's your living room looking now? Pretty awesome, right? I'm really proud of all the work you're doing, and everything you're loving away so you can have a lighter, happier life. Yay you!

WRONG ROOM

At this point, you're really making some serious progress! Well done! It's time now to take care of a bit of the 'Wrong Room' items that have been piling up. There's two ways to do this. Pick one, or try them both and then choose the one that works for you.

Option 1 – One at a time. Take one box, open it up, and grab everything you can see that goes in one room. Take those things to their proper home and put them away. No dumping things on your bed or on the table to put away later! If you don't have room to put those things away... you got it, it's time for a sort!

Say you've just grabbed 10 pairs of socks that belong in your bedroom. You head off to your bedroom, open your sock drawer... and can't put your 10 pairs away because there's no room. So, you take a few minutes to sort out the worst of your socks until there's enough room to fit the best of your socks in. Then you can toss those nasty socks and you're done. But wait! What if ALL your socks are fantastic? First of all, lucky you! You've got yourself some really nice socks! So you get to pick out a bunch of those nice ones and donate them to charity so that other people can have some nice socks too!

It's win-win – you get nice socks *and* room in your sock drawer, and other people get nice socks too!

That's pretty much what you do every time you come across a sorted space that has no more room. You pull out the worst stuff and get rid of it, or if there's only good stuff, you pull out some good stuff and donate it – just like that!

So, now that you've taken a handful of stuff to its Right Room and put it away, you head straight back to the 'Wrong Room' box and repeat. Keep doing this until the box is empty. If there's some things that go in rooms you haven't sorted yet, put them back in the box and move on.As boxes get empty you can combine them and start making some more space.

Option 2 – Big job. If you're going to try this option, give yourself at least 2 hours the first time. For this, you sort a whole bunch of Wrong Room' boxes in a row, making piles of things that go to different rooms. (Hint: make sure to label each pile so you don't forget your sorting system!) Then, you'll take each pile into its Right Room and put it away.

Again, if you don't have the space to put things away, you'll need to stop and do a sort in order to make room. You pull out the worst stuff and get rid of it, or if there's only good stuff, you pull out some good stuff and donate it – just like that!

Return to the 'Wrong Room' sorting area, and take the next pile to the next room. Keep going until all the piles are put away where they belong. If there's some things that go in rooms you haven't sorted yet, put them back in the box and move on. You don't need to do all the boxes at once here. Just work with what you feel you can manage, and enjoy the feeling of being able to take things to their rightful home and put them away!

At this point, I suspect you'll be piling up some donations. Keep taking donations in to wherever you choose. Remember **TIP #1** If you are donating things at a thrift store or charity shop *do not* go in and look around. *Do not* put a single thing back in your care. Make this a rule that you always follow.

A part of loving your clutter away is cyclical. You take things here, and then find stuff to take somewhere else, and then have things to take away, and then come back to more things that need to go somewhere else – it can feel a bit discouraging. But keep at it!

Tip #17 You are always making progress if:

- Things are leaving your house
- You are not replacing the things that leave your house AND
- Things are making their way to their Rightful Room in your home

You'll have more 'Wrong Room' things to take care of in the future, so refer back to this chapter whenever you want to make that pile smaller! Now please take 3 minutes, slow yourself down, and repeat 'I love myself' with meaning.

HALLWAYS

Yay! It's time to clear up your hallway(s) so you can walk clear through from front to back of your home. I'm excited!! You're getting so much closer to loving all your clutter away! And once the hallway(s) is done, you can have all the guests over you want (just close some doors and enjoy the company!)

Start at the front door, and work your way across the floor, sorting each item on the floor into garbage, recycling, extras/donate, illegal tenants, use it, wrong room and IDK. Keep going through each hall until all the floors are clear. Great job!!

Next go through and sort the items on shelves/stands/holders. Just focus on sorting everything from one of these areas at a time. When you have a category full (like a box/bag of 'Wrong Room') move it with the others in that category, and get a fresh container to sort into.

Remember **TIP #11** Every time you set aside a box of things you've sorted, label it clearly with a label that is certain to stay with the box. That way, when you come across it again you'll remember what it is and where it came from. You'll be surprised how much duplicate sorting this little task will save you!

Once the hallways are done, give all the floors a good vacuum. If you've decided that the hallway will no longer be used for the family to drop and leave all their stuff, make sure you tell them, and be ready for lots of reminders as they get used to the new system.

Take 3 wonderful minutes to love yourself, and really be proud of yourself and all that you're doing.

KIDS' ROOMS

Hello again! If you've skipped all the previous chapters because you can't stand your kids' room(s) and you want them cleaned up then, I'm going to stop you for a minute. I've worked with lots of parents in cluttered homes, and for many of them the first thing they want to tackle is their kids' rooms. There's 2 reasons why this isn't the best approach:

1. Your house is cluttered because you haven't been making time for yourself. You're always giving, always taking care of everyone else, but not yourself. This is the opposite of loving yourself, and it will not help you love your clutter away. Take some time to do at least 3 of the chapters, and practice lots of loving yourself before you consider your kids' rooms. If it's still important to you after that, it's Ok to switch up the order of the rooms. As long as you read this second reason too…

2. Your kids are learning from you all the time! Any parent who has accidentally let the F word slip around their kids knows how true this is. Your kids have also learned about holding on to clutter from you. So before you tell them to

clean up their stuff, you've got to start changing your own spaces, and loving your own clutter away. Trust me, you'll teach them way more with your actions than your words anyways!

Alright, if you've been working hard at loving away your clutter in the rest of the house, your kids have noticed. You're setting an amazing example to them, both about loving yourself, and about loving away your clutter. Before you begin to work with them, take some time alone to repeat 'I love myself' over and over. You'll also need a shoe box sized clear plastic container. If you don't have one, you can keep the items aside (more on that in a minute) and then put them in the container when you get one.

There's a good chance that your child is keen to be able to love away the clutter in their room. From my experience, every child is happier in a tidy, less cluttered room. Yes, every one! They may love their toys, and love creating chaos, but they really don't like living in chaos.

The most important thing here is to treat your child the way you would want to be treated – with love and kindness. You may feel frustrated during this process, but don't take it out on them. Start by telling them how much you love them. Look them in the eye when you say this. Your goal is to find out how to make your child's room feel warm and comforting to them, be easier to keep clean, and *not* be a health and safety hazard.

Start with bags/boxes labeled with the sorting categories: garbage, recycling, extras/donate, use it, wrong room, clean clothes, dirty clothes and IDK (note: there's no illegal tenants, and we've included two laundry categories). Tell them what each category means. Your goal together is to make the room a place that's nice to play and sleep in, and easy to clean up. (It may be helpful to write this down so that you both can refer to it. If your child doesn't read yet they will still appreciate the structure that the words give.) Also let them know this is a game with only one rule (and gently repeat as necessary)

Room Clean-Up Rule – Each item is a really warm (almost hot) potato, so you can only hold it for a few seconds to put it into its category.

Use the Room Clean-Up Rule to help them keep sorting and avoid playing with their toys. Even if your child is older, you can suggest this rule to help. Of course, you have to follow it too!

The clear shoe box sized container is very special. In fact, it's called a Special Bin. It will hold the most treasured things your child wants to keep for life. I know it's pretty small! But it will become important to you and your child. As you sort through the room, you may find some things that are keepers, but not actually things they use. Maybe a special baby outfit they wore, or a birthday card from Grandpa with a personal message, or a picture of their best friend from preschool who's moved away. These are things they'll treasure, and enjoy looking at over and over. As it gets full, your child (with your help) will need to sort through, and let some things go. That's OK, because the things that are *most* special will have this Special Bin to live in .

Begin sorting the things on the floor at the door one at a time. Talk to them as you work together. You can sort as well, but ask them before you choose a category for something. Even most 'Use it' items. Kids can be much more willing to let things go than their parents. Of course, things like clothes they wear, and school things are automatically kept, so these can be sorted without permission *but* you could be talking about what you're doing as you go.

The degree that your child can sort on their own depends on their age and personality. You'll have to be flexible in your approach so you can be the most supportive to them. If the room is quite cluttered, celebrate every time another section of floor is cleared. If you can get across the floor fairly easily, make sure to celebrate when the floor is clear.

Once you've cleared the floor, go together to put any full bags of garbage, recycling, and donate away. Through all of this you're teaching them how to clean up, so make sure they can do each step.

It's a good idea to take them with you when you donate things as well, and help them understand how their donations help people. Remember **TIP #1** If you are donating things at a thrift store or charity shop *do not* go in and look around. *Do not* put a single thing back in your care. Make this a rule that you always follow.

While you want to keep working at the room, you'll also need to take breaks when it's necessary. It can be hard to find the balance between learning to stick to something, and not pushing too hard. Do your best, and always be kind and loving. When you take a break, give a clear time that you'll come back to it. Timers are great for this. And a little snack always helps too.

Once the floor is clear, let's head to the closet. If there are things that are in their proper place here, and are definite 'Use it's' then leave them here. Everything else gets sorted into categories. As you work together, decide what will go in the closet. Clothes that hang up, of course. Maybe a basket for dirty laundry (without a lid, to make it easy to toss things in), folded clothes on the shelves, shoes on the floor, certain large toys…. It really depends on what your child will be keeping, and the set-up of the closet. What's important is that they have easy-to-follow rules for where *everything* goes.

Sort through everything in the closet, and put back the things that belong. If it helps, put some sticky notes up as a reminder of what belongs in the closet. Continue to the dresser. First clear off the top. Sort each item. If you find things that go in the closet, put them away. Once the top is clear, give it a wipe. Decide together what will live on the dresser. Remember to look for things they use nearly every day, and a few things that make them happy to look at.

Now let's move on to the drawers. As you did in your bedroom, label the drawers with what you think should go in them. Start with the first drawer. Take everything out and sort into categories (garbage, recycling, extras/donate, illegal tenants, use it, wrong room and IDK for anything that's not clothes), and then sort the clothing into the categories you've labeled on the drawers.

Pull out anything that's too small, stained, worn out, or things you know your child never wears. (The exception here is if your child really wants to keep something and thinks they'll wear it.) Put anything back that belongs in the drawer you just sorted, and move to the next drawer. Keep repeating this until each drawer has been sorted and the clothes have been put where they belong.

As you did in the rest of the house, if you can't fit everything in a drawer, sort it again, and be more particular about what you keep. This is a great opportunity for you and your child to practice keeping your things within reasonable boundaries. It will also make it *way* easier for them to find their clothes, and put their clean clothes away on laundry day.

When the dresser is finished, move to the top of the bed. Again, take each item off, sort it into categories, and put things away when you can. Once the bed is cleared, make it. Hopefully you have bedding that's easy for your child to tidy themselves. Try to get them in the habit of making their bed every morning when they get up – just like you do!

Once the bed is clear, take a break if you need one. Tell your child how much you love them, tell yourself how much you love you, and then eat a snack, go for a walk, read a story, or even take a break from each other if you need.

When you return, take a minute to point out everything your child has done, and what a great job they're doing. Make sure they know that a tidy room with less stuff is easier to take care of (so they have more time to do fun things!)

Let's move to the bedside table next. Start with the top. Clear it off, sort each item one at a time, and then give the cleared surface a wipe. Again, put things back that are used nearly every day, and maybe one thing that makes your child smile. Move to the drawers/shelves of the side table. If there are drawers here, they *don't* have to be perfectly organized. Definitely sort through all the items and get rid of garbage and excess, but then make easy categories (like craft stuff, stickers, toy cars…) so they can have a spot for the things they play with most. Label the drawers with a picture/word to help them remember. Tell them how much you love them and what a great job they're doing!

OK, now it's time for the real excavating to begin – we're going under the bed! Have your child take things out one at a time, and tell you what category each belongs in. No matter what they unearth under there, don't get crazy upset. The important thing is that they're taking care of their clutter. You can certainly clarify what is, and isn't OK to keep/shove/hide under the bed, but do it calmly. Hey, at least you found all that food before it became its own habitat....

The best plan is to store nothing under the bed from now on. If nothing belongs under there, then it's pretty hard to get away with shoving things there when it's room cleaning time! However, sometimes it really is the best place for some bulky items. Things like a suitcase, large musical instrument, racetrack set, or even a box of Lego might do well to have a special, accessible home under the bed.

Ready for the last frontier in the bedroom? It's the toys. Trust me when I tell you that kids are not happier with more toys. Yes, they're happier when they *get* more toys, but they are not happier when they *have* more toys. This may be hard for you, especially if you grew up without toys, or you show love by giving gifts. If you need to, step back from the bedroom and love yourself. Think back to the child you were, and love that little one. Then, think with gratitude on the life you have with your own child now. Separate the child you were from the child you have. You love them both, but your child cannot live out the life you wished for. When you step back into the room, focus on being present with your child right now. Let's make a calm, less cluttered life for them where they can enjoy hanging out with the awesome parent you are!

So, gather all the toys together and let's do another sort. Here are the categories:

- Baby Toys (toys they've out grown)
- Growing Into Toys (toys they can't use yet, but want to in the future)

- Broken/old/out of date Toys
- Bits and Pieces (parts to everything and anything)
- Top 10 (their 10 most favorite best in the world toys)
- Use It (toys they'd like to keep)

Baby toys need to be donated or put away for the next sibling. If they have a favorite toy or two they still want to keep, this is great. It's a way of remembering their childhood as they grow up. Keep these safe, but stored in their room.

Growing Into Toys also need to be stored in their room if at all possible. Make sure to label the box/bag/bin, and put a reminder in your phone to check these Growing Into Toys in 6 months. No use keeping them if they're forgotten about until your child's too old for them.

Broken/old/out of date Toys should be put in the garbage, or donated if they're still good quality. Remember **Tip #9** It's good to donate, but only donate good stuff!

Bits and Pieces can go in their own labelled container for now. Add/remove as you find where they belong, or find other pieces. When you check the Growing Into Toys in 6 months, take a quick check through the Bits and Pieces. Things that have not found their home/use can be tossed.

Top 10 toys get put in special, accessible homes so your child can play with them and put them back daily. It's really important to focus on these favorites, as it helps them (and you) identify what toys they really enjoy the most.

Use It toys can be put away, but remember your limits. If the toy bin/shelf/whatever is full and the toys don't all fit you'll need to have another sort so you can easily put things away.

Wow! What a job, hey? Chances are, you'll be repeating this process for a few years, but you'll become less involved as your child gains the skills to sort things themselves, and gets in the habit of putting things away.

Now, either your child is beginning you to play in their lovely new clean room, or you both need a change of scenery. If they want to play, that's great! Just remind them they'll need to bring the room back to its tidy place after playing – and be sure to follow through. If you both need a change, do something to celebrate. Some time at the park, watching a show together, or anything else to reward yourselves. You've done it! You've worked with your child to clean their room, but, much more importantly, you're giving them life skills so that one day they'll do a great job of managing their own home!

HOME OFFICE

The home office…a blessing and a curse all wrapped up into one room! It's so nice to have a separate space for an office, and so awful to have a room that collects everything and anything, whether it's for the office or not!

The goal in your office is to isolate any critical paperwork, create a space to hold the paperwork you will be sorting at another date, decide what items you will store in your office, and clear everything else out. Of course, you'll be loving yourself all the time, so take 3 minutes to warm up by saying 'I love myself' with meaning.

Let's start on the floor. Begin clearing a 1 foot wide path to the desk. Sort each item one at a time into garbage, recycling, extras/donate, illegal tenants, use it, wrong room and IDK, and two new categories: paperwork and critical paperwork. Critical paperwork must be dealt with or you will face serious consequences. Bills, taxes, and time-dependent forms are critical. Pretty much everything else is just plain old paperwork.

Clear off the top of the desk, sorting each item into the categories. Once the desk surface is clear, wipe it clean. Enjoy how nice that looks! Place the critical paperwork on top of the desk. If there are some critical items you can quickly take care of (less than 5 minutes per item), go ahead and take care of these.

Take 3 minutes to love yourself out loud. You are now clearing clutter *and* dealing with important stuff that's been secretly bugging you – great job!!

Remembering that critical paperwork can now be placed on the desk, continue clearing the floor by working from the edge of your cleared path in a counter clockwise direction. Pick up each item one at a time and sort it into garbage, recycling, extras/donate, illegal tenants, use it, wrong room, IDK, and paperwork. I'm so excited for you!! It's going to feel fantastic to have this room working properly as your home office!!

When the floor is clear (Woohoo!) take a break. Get a snack, go for a walk, do a little dance, just something to give you a break from seeing pens and paper for a bit.

Ready for the next step? Let's take care of the rest of your desk. The top is clear except for your pile of critical paperwork (YAY!). If you have a pen holder, you can leave this on the desk too, but make sure it has no more than 6 of your very best pens/pencils/highlighters on it. This is really important!

Most clutterers have suffered a shortage of writing instruments in their past, and feel a nearly irresistible urge to hoard vast amounts of pens and pencils. More than they can possibly use in a lifetime (I'm not exaggerating here). It may seem like a small thing, but when you have to dig through pens in every drawer to find something, it starts to cost you time. Instead, keep your best pens and pencils easily accessible on your desk, keep an equal number as back-up (easily accessible *in* your desk), and get rid of all the rest.

Don't worry, even if you get down to a dozen of your best pens and pencils, you're still going to find more in your home!

OK, so back to your desk. Start with the first drawer closest to your hands when you are at your desk. This is where you want to keep things you frequently use. Sort everything in it one at a time, and put back items you're always looking for. Scissors, tape, stapler, staple remover, chapstick. Whatever it is you tend to waste time looking for when you're working at your desk, put in this drawer as long as it all fits in easily. If you've never actually had the chance to work at your desk, just put in the things you think you'll use, and you can adjust later as needed.

Now, let's label the rest of the drawers in a similar way to how you labelled the drawers in your bedroom dresser. Think of the things you'd like to keep handy in these drawers, and put labels up. This is not a fixed system. You can change and switch around as you find out what you need. Possible labels could be 'Mailing supplies', 'Extra paper', Filing supplies', 'Office supplies' or 'Important cords and chargers'.

Sort through one drawer at a time, putting back the items you want in that drawer and putting the rest of the items on the desk (if they will go in another drawer as you sort) or in the right category (garbage, recycling, extras/donate, illegal tenants, use it, wrong room and IDK). Remember, if you can't fit things easily in a drawer, re-sort the items and remove things that are not the best. You must be able to easily put things in each drawer – and take them out when needed. This is the trick to keeping your space tidy.

TIP #18 – It's easier to keep things tidy when you can easily take them out when you need them and easily put them back when you're done.

Once your desk is clean and shiny and organized, give yourself a few moments to bask in the sunshine breaking out over your head. What an amazing accomplishment!!! Take 3 minutes to remind yourself how much you love you!!

If you have a filing cabinet in your office, go ahead and clean out the top, but leave the contents – we'll tackle the papers inside when it's paperwork time. Oh, that's unless you have drawers that don't contain paperwork. Those can be sorted and cleared out.

Any other furniture type items in your office also need to be sorted and cleared. Remember to only put things on top of a surface if you use them nearly every day, or if you love looking at them (but only a few of these). If you have a bookshelf, you only need to sort and clear until all the books you have in your office fit easily onto the shelf. If you know you have books in your 'Wrong Room' boxes that you'll want to keep, you can work to have some clear spaces on your bookshelf to make it easier to put things away.

Books are another category that many clutterers have in common. They represent information – something clutterers love! But even the noblest of books works against you if it contributes to a space that is too full. When you sort books, start with any that are clearly out of date. Let those ones go.

Next, get rid of books that make you feel bad, or guilty. Books that you 'should' read, books that tell you how to be someone you're not, books about parenting you never read, and now your kids are adults. Those can all take their negativity and leave. When you come across anything that brings negative feelings, take 3 minutes and repeat out loud 'I love myself'. Don't let those negative feelings interfere with your life, and your ability to love your clutter away.

Finish up with any areas in your office that need to be tackled. Follow the method of sorting each item into categories (garbage, recycling, extras/donate, illegal tenants, use it, wrong room and IDK), putting back the things that belong in that area, and doing a re-sort if you cannot *easily* put things back, continuing to love your clutter away until you can put it away easily.

OK, I don't know how long this took you, but home offices are a BIG job, and you did it!!!! You are amazing!! Take 3 minutes to tell yourself how amazing you are!!

The last thing to do is to collect all the boxes/bags of paperwork and stack them neatly against one wall in your home office. This will be their home from now on. Just one more room to clean, and then you'll get to start taking care of the paperwork.

SPARE ROOM

For most people, spare rooms are a great idea...until they get used as a dumping ground! It's just too easy to dump things in the spare room when you don't know where they go, or you just don't feel like putting them away.

It's OK to have many purposes for your spare room – even storing things. But everything must have a home, and things that don't belong, well, they shouldn't live here.

You do need to take a few minutes and decide *what* you will keep in here. Some common categories are hobby/craft supplies, luggage, gift wrapping supplies, and holiday decorations. It really can be just about anything as long as:

- You actually use them
- They fit in the space <u>easily</u>
- You don't have to move them in order to accommodate a guest

Once you've decided what will live in your guest room, you can get started. Clear a 1 foot pathway from the door to the bed. Sort each item one at a time into the categories garbage, recycling, extras/donate, illegal tenants, use it, wrong room and IDK. Remember, 'Use It' is for things you intend to keep in the guest room.

Once you've cleared a path to the bed, clear off the bed by sorting each item on at a time. If you can, make the bed. If the bedding needs a wash, you might want to run it though the washer and dryer while you're loving the clutter away in the rest of the room, but this is up to you. If you're right into the flow of things, keep going!

Finish clearing the floor by sorting each item one at a time. Working from your path, move in a counter clockwise direction around your room. Be sure to clear out the things *under* the bed as well. Who knows, you might even find last year's Christmas presents that you forgot you bought!

TIP #18 If you *do* find gifts you bought and forgot at any time during your sorting, make sure you label them who you bought them for. Then, place a reminder in your phone or in your calendar for 3 weeks before you would give it to them. (For example, if you found Christmas gifts, put a reminder in your phone at the beginning of December that says 'Christmas gifts are under the spare room bed (or wherever they are)' or 'Mother's Day gift is in closet'. Choose one place in your home to store gifts, and label every one with whom it's for. Never buy a gift unless it is intended for someone specific.

When the floor is clear, move to the bedside table and clear it. Leave it completely clear, or with the very minimum. Maybe a lamp, a clock, and something nice to look at. Do the same for the dresser. As in the past, label each drawer with what you think you'll store in it. Since this is the spare room, keep a top drawer empty for guests to use. Remember that you can only store what will easily fit in the rest of the drawers. Continue to love your clutter away until you can do this.

In the closet, leave a half dozen empty hangers with at least a foot of space for guests to hang things. Again, make sure that the things you choose to store here will easily fit, and are easily accessible when you want to use them.

If there's any other furniture/storage in the room, sort through everything on and in it using the same methods. Try to keep tops and surfaces clear except for a few things that are nice to look at.

When you're done the guest room, take a step back and admire the progress! You're really getting ready to welcome good things into your life now! Well done! Be ready to use this room for its purpose – welcoming people into your home.

PAPERWORK

We've made it to the paperwork chapter! There's a reason it's so far into the book. It's given you a chance to round up paperwork throughout your home so that you can tackle the majority of it at once. If you have a home office, head over there. If you don't have a home office, you'll probably want to do this at your dining room. Isn't it nice that your table is clear so you have room? Yay for you!!

Everyone will have different categories with their paperwork, and different priorities that need to be addressed. I'll be as specific as possible, but only use the advice that's helpful to you.

First Pass

To begin, you'll need some supplies. Chances are you've found lots of office supplies through your sorting. If not, it's OK to purchase what you need, but watch out! Office supply stores promise you a world of organization if you'll only buy all those gorgeous items. THEY LIE!! The more you buy, the more you have clutter. So only purchase the absolute basics, no matter how 'useful' everything else looks.

Here's what you need (*if* you don't already have these)

- File folders
- Hanging file folders
- Labels for hanging file folders
- Stapler
- You'll also need something to hold your files if you don't have a file cabinet. You can buy a box designed to hold hanging files from any office store if you're looking for the most cost effective method. Unless you have your own business, you need two standard drawers for your files *or less*.
- You might also want to get a paper shredder.

Alright, so let's get started. At this point you can be at your desk, or your dining room table. Have the surface cleared off so you have lots of room to work. Also have an empty box/bag at your feet for recycling, one for garbage, and one for shredding.

Take 3 minutes to say out loud 'I love myself'. Really mean it. Loving yourself makes everything better – even paperwork!

We're going to take care of the paperwork in stages. The first stage is a basic sort. When I'm working with clients we sometimes call it a 'first pass'. You're going to sort all the paperwork into 4 categories: Critical paperwork, general paperwork, shredding, and recycling. (The trash is just there in case you come across some garbage.) As you've done in the past, critical paperwork is things that must be dealt with promptly to avoid serious consequences. General paperwork is all other paperwork you choose to keep. Shredding is for any papers you're not keeping that contain sensitive information. And of course, recycling is for all other paper.

Please note **TIP #19** Your name and address are *not* private or sensitive information! It's publicly available, and there is not benefit to you in shredding papers that have your name and address. Do not waste time shredding papers only because your name and address are on them.

Put two pieces of paper/sticky notes on your table. On one write Critical, and on the other write General. Now you're ready to get started! Take the first box/bag of paperwork, and open it up. Take out the first piece of paper and put it into critical paperwork, general paperwork, shredding, or recycling. (It's up to you whether you shred as you go, or run a pile of papers through the shredder every once in a while. Just make sure that if you do have shredding you finish it at the end of each sorting session.)

Your goal here is to get all the papers into one of the four categories quickly. Don't get distracted reading things. If you're not sure, place it in general paperwork and move on. If you have things in envelopes, open them up, and if you choose to keep them, staple them together and recycle the envelope. Don't put papers you're keeping back into their envelopes, it just takes extra time later on to take them out again.

Once you've sorted a box/bag, take a short break. Stand up, maybe empty the recycling or run papers through the shredder. Get some fresh air, grab a snack, and come back for some more fun! (OK, it may be more fun for someone like me, but it'll be fun to have it done, right?)

Keep going with your sorting. Move as quickly as possible but don't panic or rush. You just want to avoid getting distracted by papers. If you come across magazines and newsletters, only keep them if they're a current issue. You *know* you won't actually read all the past issues, so let them go now before they clutter up your brain any more.

After each box/bag take a break, and remember to keep loving yourself! You're getting stuff <u>done</u> that's been hanging over your head for a loooong time. Be proud of yourself!

Once the paperwork has all had its first sort, you will likely have a small critical pile, a general pile, and hopefully lots of recycled and shredded paperwork. Great job!! Go ahead and return the general paperwork to one of the boxes you were using. Label it very clearly

'Sorted Paper to Keep'. Make sure all your shredding is done, and take out the recycling, shredding, and any garbage.

Now it's time to take care of the critical paperwork. Deal with everything you can. If there's something that will take a significant amount of time (like taxes), keep it close, but take care of anything else you can first. Once a critical item has been taken care of, it's no longer critical (Yay!) and can go into the general paperwork box.

Filing System

Now that you've identified the paperwork you think you'll keep, it's time to give it a home that makes it *easy* to find things when you need them, and *easy* to put things away. This is going to take some time, but once you've set up a good system, you only need to maintain it, and tweak it as your life and needs change.

Here's how it works:

Hanging Folders – these are used for broad categories, such as Money, Taxes, Vehicle, Home.

Labels for Hanging Folders – these plastic tabs with paper inserts will be used to label *every* hanging folder.

File Folders – these are used for more specific categories that will fit inside the hanging folders. You will write on each file folder the label for what's in it.

TIP #20 Any organizing system only works if it works for <u>YOU</u>. When you choose categories or labels, pick the first word that comes to mind. This is most likely to be the word that you will think of first the next time you're looking for your item. For example, 'Vehicle', 'Car', 'Toyota', and 'Mindy' (or whatever you name your car) all mean the same thing, but only one of them will be the right label for things related to your car.

Get out the paper labels that fit into the plastic tabs for your hanging folders. You're going to start with some basic categories to get you started on filing. (Even if you already have a filing set-up, you may want to start this process from the beginning to ensure it's set up in the best way for you. It can be easier to start fresher than using an old system.)

You may want to write in pencil to start so you can change things if you want to. Start with a tab for money, one for your vehicle(s), one for insurance, one for bills, one for taxes and one for health/medical. *Remember: Choose a title that makes sense to you. If 'Finances' works better for you than money, or some other word, then please use it.

Once you have these labels made, put them into hanging folders, and hang the folders in the box/file drawer you have ready. Always hang in alphabetical order (bills, health, insurance, money, vehicle).

Now you can get going on finding home for your papers! Pick up the first paper. What comes to mind when you look at it? For example, if you've picked up a bank statement, you might think 'Checking account' or the name of your bank. Whichever comes to mind, write the title on a file folder, and then place that file folder in the 'Money' hanging file. Isn't this fun? Now, every time you come across another bank statement, you know exactly where it goes! Easy!

Keep going, one paper at a time. If it fits into one of the hanging file categories you've already made, put it in a labeled file folder and then into the hanging file. Of course, you're going to have to make some new main categories as you go along. Here's some suggestions:

- If you have paper for family members (children, spouse), make a hanging file for each of them with their names on the label. The folders inside this hanging file might say 'School', 'Health', 'Certificates' – really anything that fits with their life.
- If a family member has a lot of papers, such as a child who's had lots of medical treatments, then you can start a second hanging file just for this. Label it with their name, and the word medical (ie. Carmen – Medical). Inside, the file folders can be separated by doctor, treatment type, lab reports –

whatever will make it easy to locate information when you need it.

- Your circumstances will guide your filing. If you only have one credit card, you may want to put it in the 'Money' hanging file. If you have multiple credit cards, you may want to set-up a hanging file for 'Credit Cards'.
- You can set up hanging file categories for anything that suits you. Our family travels quite a bit, so we have a hanging file that says 'Travel Documents' and it contains our travelling documents in an easy-to-grab folder.
- If you have lots of magazine cuttings, consider switching to Pinterest. You can pin all the beautiful pictures and helpful guides you want online, and it will never clutter your desk again. (Plus, it might actually make it possible to find a certain recipe when you're looking for it!)
- If you have multiple vehicles with lots of paperwork you want to keep, it may be easier to have a hanging file for each vehicle. Inside you'll have folders for maintenance, registration, etc.
- If you have a lot of papers for taxes (especially if you run your own business), you may need to have a drawer/box just for these. Once the taxes are filed, past years can each be put into a hanging file with the year. For your current year, have a few file folders in this year's tax hanging file for things like expenses, income, and donations. If you're in Canada, you're expected to keep 7 years of tax info. Shred everything older than that, except your summaries, or any open disputes. In the States you're expected to keep 3 years of tax info. Beyond this, check with state and federal requirements for what to keep and how long.
- Other helpful hanging file categories might include
- House maintenance
- Warranties and Receipts for Big Purchases (Honest, it works!)
- Happy Thoughts (cards and notes that make you smile)
- Watch out for coupons!! I have not yet met a clutterer that

can keep their coupons managed well, but I've met a lot of clutterers that love to keep every coupon they can get their hands on. Unless you have the time and inclination to set up a coupon management strategy and keep up with it, then coupons are causing more chaos than the money they might save.

Remember **TIP #10** At any time if you are feeling like you just can't do anymore, remember that it's OK to stop. You're doing something that's very different than what you're used to and it can take some time to get in the groove. Always end a loving your clutter away session by taking three minutes to say 'I love myself' out loud. Then, make sure the area you were working on is left safe, take all your sorted categories to their homes, and give yourself a well-deserved break!

As you're able to, continue sorting through papers one at a time, and putting them into labelled folders, which you then put into the correct labelled hanging file. For the most part, try to stick to the categories that come to mind first. There will probably be some times when you'll need to change things a bit – getting more specific when the category is too general, and creating a more general category so you don't have twenty folders that each have 2 papers in them.

Every time you put away all the papers from a bag/box, celebrate!!! It's a really big deal, and you need to be really, really proud of yourself!! I'm proud of you too!!

Once you've created lovely home folder for your papers, and you've put them all in their place, your job is not done. The thing about papers is that they're going to keep coming into your home. And unfortunately, the one-in-one-out rule doesn't quite work for papers! So, you're going to be spending some quality time with your files on a pretty regular basis.

How do you keep up with paperwork? Excellent question! Here are some tips:

Tip #21 Managing paperwork

- Open all your mail every day. Immediately recycle junk and unnecessary papers.
- Separate critical paperwork from general paperwork. Any critical paperwork that can be easily dealt with can be handled right away and then sent to the general paperwork pile.
- Keep a highlighter where you open mail. Highlight due dates and action points.
- Regularly file your general paperwork. The more often you file it, the less time it will take.
- Twice a year go through every paper in your files. This is a quick pass through to find things that are no longer necessary and remove them. I once heard someone refer to this as 'grooming' your files. It's just like getting a little trim to keep things tidy. Choose times of the year that are not as busy, and that make sense to you, and then put a reminder on your phone and in your calendar.

Managing your paperwork will make your house tidier, your finances better, your documents safer, and your stress level lower. It's win win win!!! Keep up with it, and enjoy all the time you save by being so fantastically organized!

THE GARAGE

Garages… the last frontier for chaos and clutter. It's truly ironic that so many people park their $30,000 car in the driveway because their garage is full of $400 worth of clutter! And I've lost count of the number of people I know who get asked "Are you having a garage sale?" every time they open their garages. Time to make good use of that space you're paying for with every single rent/mortgage payment. Garages were designed to hold cars, and they did – when we all had less stuff.

In the garage we're going to use a slightly different strategy for loving away clutter. As always, take time before you start to love yourself. Remember to mean it when you say, 'I love myself'!

Next, at whatever angle you can get at them, start grabbing cardboard boxes and flattening them. You can put a few aside to re-use, but no more than 10. The truth is, many of you are saving cardboard boxes that you might need one day, and these boxes are taking up space where items you've bought with your hard-earned money could be safely stored instead. Ditch the boxes folks, they're stopping you from enjoying your space!

Once you've grabbed and flattened all those boxes, you may need to take a drive to the recycling depot. Since you need all the free space you can get, it's worth it to make this trip. Remember **TIP #2** Don't wait until you have 'enough' or a full load of anything you're getting rid of. You will be more successful getting 3 things gone this week than saving 200 things to get rid of next year.

Next, let's pull out any garbage and recycling you can get your hands on. If you can gather a pile, it will help create space in your garage. You may to haul this stuff away as well – your neighbors, your spouse, and your sanity will thank you.

Now it's time to start clearing a path. Begin at the entrance you use to access your garage (or, if you can only get in through the big garage door, open it and start at the spot closest your home entrance). Clear a 2 foot wide path from here to the next entrance/exit from your garage.

Yep, you're clearing a wider path than you have in the past. This is because there's so many bulky things in garages that having a wider path will make your whole job more efficient.

Once you've cleared a 2 foot path from one entrance to another entrance, start with the edge of the path closest to a wall, and begin working to clear the floor to the wall. Sort each item one at a time into garbage, recycling, extras/donate, illegal tenants, use it, wrong room and IDK. Remember that the 'Use it' category is for things that you would like to keep in the garage.

It might be a bit crowded at first as you're sorting. To help with this, take out garbage and recycling as soon as you have a bag/box full. Make sure it's easy to tell which category is which, so piles don't end up merging back together – that would be annoying because then you'd have to re-sort things!

When you've got this section of the garage cleared, go ahead and put away any 'Use it' items that belong in this area. (Did you catch that? You already have a clear space in the garage to start using – that's amazing! You're amazing!) If you're not sure where things will go, you can wait to put things away. In general, you want to store things you will need access from the house near the door to the house, and things for your vehicle closer to where your vehicle will park.

Take 3 minutes to love yourself, and congratulate yourself on loving the clutter away in your garage! Some people never get their garages cleared out – but you're doing it right now!

Most of your storage will happen along the walls, so as you clear these spaces you'll be making room to put the things you'll actually be keeping in the garage. When you've made a space for something, go ahead and put it there.

I know this is a slow process and a big job. Take breaks as you need, and always love yourself first, last, and in-between. Remember **TIP #10** At any time if you are feeling like you just can't do anymore, remember that it's OK to stop. You're doing something that's very different than what you're used to and it can take some time to get in the groove. Always end a loving your clutter away session by taking three minutes to say 'I love myself' out loud. Then, make sure the area you were working on is left safe, take all your sorted categories to their homes, and give yourself a well-deserved break!

So, back to the garage. The process here is to continue to make a 2 foot path towards the next door, and then clear your clutter one item at a time from the path to the wall. Every time you clear an area you will be using for storage, go ahead and place the right items into their homes. Since so many garage items are large, this will set you up well to have an orderly space.

As you're clearing, think about what activities you'll actually be doing in the garage. This is different from the activities you *want* to be doing in the garage! It's so easy to get caught up in garage fanta-syland, but if you do it will be hard to create spaces for the things you'll actually be doing.

If you've never fixed anything in your life, you won't need a great deal of tools for fixing things. But if you used to fix things regularly, and you want to do this again, then you can have fun setting up your tools and space for fixing things.

Maybe you really only need space for storing your sports gear and your truck. So your focus will be on clearing space to easily get at all your gear, and be able to drive your truck in and out of the garage without running over your golf clubs.

If you have a whole bunch of things you want to do and have in your garage, decide how much space each will take. Add room to walk around everything and park your vehicle. Can you do it? If you can, great! But if not, you'll need to choose the most important ones to you. There aren't many people in the world who have a garage big enough to do *everything* in. So you're in good company if you have to work in the space you have!

Now, what about all the non-garage items that have made their way into your garage? Two things:

1. When the rest of your house is cleared of clutter, you'll have room for most things in the rooms where they belong.
2. If your house and garage have been full of clutter, it's time to love a good part of that clutter away so you have room to live easily and comfortably.

Having room in your house for the things you need *and* loving away clutter will help you have a garage that isn't overflowing. You'll be able to easily get in and out of your garage, and use the things you want to use without spending an hour looking for it!

Once you've found homes for things you're keeping inside your home, and loved lots of clutter away, you may need some storage space in the garage, but not much. Often garages are used for non-garage things like seasonal items, camping gear, suitcases. This is just fine when you have a reasonable amount (20 bins of Christmas gear is not reasonable, unless you're charging admission for tours during Christmas). If you're storing things that will only be used once a year, they can be less accessible. You can even use the rafters to store bins and large items if you're able to get them in and out yourself.

There's a large group of clutterers that have a large amount of tools.

So, here's a few words about tools... Some people really really love tools. Love tools, all tools, need tools, lots and lots of tools. While it's completely true that jobs are much easier to do when you have the right tools, it's also true that if you have too many tools you'll rarely find the right tool when you need it.

The goal is to have enough tools to get the major jobs done easily (well, as easy as major jobs can be), and not have to shuffle through piles of tools to find the ones you need. I know, it's much easier said than done! But if you keep it in your mind that having extra tools makes it harder to find what you need, you'll start to be more aware of the tools that add to clutter instead of making the job easier.

As much as possible, have tools stored up on the wall, or in chests with shallow drawers where you can see each tool in the drawer. Deep boxes hide tools, spiders, and sharp objects, and you always find the spiders and sharp objects before you find the tools.

Let's take a minute to review: You've made a 2 foot wide path between each entrance in your garage, and then cleared the space from the path to the walls. You've put away some items in their proper spaces, and you're starting to have some good ideas about what you'll be using your garage for. There's probably just one thing left...

The big pile in the middle of your garage. I know how daunting this can feel, but you've made the whole job way easier by giving yourself big, clear paths out of your garage! Just like when you started loving away your garage clutter, start with the cardboard boxes. Because now that you've cleared a path, you can get at more cardboard! You've already set aside some good boxes, so grab the rest, flatten them, and take them to the recycling depot if they won't fit in your recycling can.

Next, are there any items you know are garbage? Things like the cracked kiddie pool you were going to turn into a vegetable garden, your dad's bent golf clubs, that couch you were going to reupholster... Pull these things out and send them on their merry way to the dump. Take any other garbage and recycling away as well. Remember, if you need to take a break, first make the area safe, take any sorted categories to their homes, and say 'I love myself' a few times before taking your well-deserved break.

If you have a garage full of things you had planned to fix/repurpose, then you need to set a plan that you can follow. Don't worry about all the things you didn't fix. You kept them because you're a creative and resourceful thinker, and that type of thinking says a lot about the interesting person you are! But I know you'll feel much better about fixing one thing a month than you will feel about collecting hundreds of things you never fix.

So as you're loving your clutter away, pick two or three things that you *really* think it would be <u>fun</u> to fix. Fun is the key word here! Don't even think about picking things you *should* fix – don't! Never, never *should* on yourself. Instead, focus on what really makes you feel excited to fix. And keep your 'fix it' inventory to three or less. If you find that you're using your new, organized garage to fix more things, then you can up this number a bit. But focus on what you actually fix. Then you can have the satisfaction of saying 'I fixed that', instead of being embarrassed about how much broken stuff is piled in your garage.

When you're ready, take a minute to notice the shrinking pile. Great job! Now it's a matter of steadily taking one item at a time, putting it in its category, and repeating. When the category is full, take it away to its home, and start a new box/bag for it. When you find things that belong in the garage, put them in their homes whenever possible. It may take a while, but steady at it gets the job done.

Once you've loved the clutter away in your garage, you really need to celebrate! However you party, now's the time because you've done the (nearly) impossible!!! Woooohoooo!!

OK, a few final things about your super awesome garage. Always think about the easiest way to keep things tidy and organized. Neat little jars hanging from their lids look great on Pinterest, but if it's more likely that you'll put your bits and bobs away if they're in open jars on a shelf, then do that instead.

If you found you had lots of garbage and recycling when you cleared your garage, then make sure you have the right sized cans easily accessible so you'll actually use them, and empty them as needed.

Keep the tools you're always using in a place you can easily grab them, and put them back. And always put them back. No job is done unless the tools are safely stored, and everything is cleaned up. And having a job done feels reeeaaallly good, so go ahead and put those tools away!

As your life, hobbies, and needs change, the layout of your garage may change. Just pay a bit of attention to what gets used in your garage and what doesn't. Useless things can be loved away to make room for useful things that represent the life you're living right now.

Oh, and when you drive your car into your garage every night and you see your neighbor staring in awe? Go ahead and feel a little smug. You really are fantastic and you know it.

CRAFT ROOMS

Before we work on your craft room, take 3 minutes to say 'I love myself' over and over. Feel that love reaching all the way down to your toes, and filling you up with happiness. Such a good feeling, right?

If you have a craft room, then you see yourself as a crafter... or a scrapbooker, or a painter, or a quilter. The idea of creating makes you feel happy, and you love collecting all the tools and supplies that go along with creating. You may even be thinking that you're going to get lots of creating done when you have an organized craft/sewing/scrapbooking/creating room.

There's something I've noticed over and over with clutterers who love creating...It's more fun buying supplies than doing projects. So, I want you to think about whether you create lots, or have a creative mind. There's a difference. Now that you're loving yourself (and doing such a good job of it!), you can take a look at your actions, and think about how much creating you do.

Of course, creating can be difficult for clutterers who are constrained by crowded spaces, hidden supplies, and projects that get forgotten in the piles. But in order to create a craft space you're going to use, you'll need to think realistically about what type of craft you'll be doing. I recommend starting with just one craft. Even though you're completely able to *think* about so many fantastic crafty things to do, you'll still only be able to *do* one at a time.

Best option is to stick to one craft, and sort everything else into donate. Can you commit to this? It will really free up your space and your time. But, if one just isn't enough, have a subcategory craft that you will keep supplies for safely stored in two clear bins <u>or less</u>.

So, when you start sorting, any tools and supplies that fit this second craft will be sorted into your two (or less) bins. If you have more than what will fit into two bins, do another sort until you can fit everything within your boundaries. This will make sure that you've created space for your number one crafting choice. If you haven't opened these bins after a year, just donate them without blinking an eye.

Ready to get started? Let's go! Make sure you have boxes/bags for each of your categories: garbage, recycling, extras/donate, illegal tenants, use it, wrong room and IDK. If you are keeping supplies for a second craft, have your clear bins ready and sort right into these bins.

Begin at the door to the craft room. Work on making a 1 foot wide path from the door to your workstation/craft table. Start sorting items one at a time into your categories. When a bag/box is full, take it to its home, or as close to its home as you can get. (For example, garbage could go straight into your garbage bin, but donate might be put at your front door or in your car.)

When you come across items you've had for a long time – and never used – let them go. Your craft space will feel much more inspiring and inviting when you have fresh things to look at that don't bring up feelings of guilt or regret. This will also apply to just-started or half-completed projects.

Tip #21 You are NOT obligated to finish everything you start. Get rid of projects that are not a good fit for your current life. This includes projects that are too difficult, expired (baby toys for your now-teenager), make you feel guilty every time you look at them, or you just don't want to do.

So, as you're making the path from your door to your workstation/craft table you're removing garbage, recycling, extras/donate, illegal tenants, use it, wrong room and IDK. You're also letting go of craft supplies for everything except your first choice, and maybe a second choice of craft. If you are keeping a second choice of supplies you're immediately sorting them into two clear plastic bins that will be your measure of how much you're keeping. Finally, you're also letting go of projects you've started and won't be finishing. Taking these steps will make a big difference in your progress as you love your clutter away!

Once you've made it your workstation, celebrate! Way to go! Take 3 minutes to love yourself in your newly cleared pathway. If you're ready to continue, take away any bags/boxes of sorting that are full, and get some fresh bags ready to keep going.

The next step is to clear your workstation/craft table. You want to make this a beautiful, welcoming surface that holds only a few often-used supplies and maybe a light. Of course if you primarily sew, your sewing machine may have a home here too. Even though you still have the rest of the room to work through, having a clear workstation surface will help the whole space to feel better, and you'll be itching to get the room done so you can start crafting (which is exactly the point!)

Remember your categories as your sorting: garbage, recycling, extras/donate, illegal tenants, use it, wrong room, IDK, and first craft category. When the workstation is clear, wipe it clean, set up your often-used supplies, and enjoy!

Next, clear a 1 foot wide path from your workstation to the main closet/dresser/shelf/storage in the room. Keep going with your categories. Be sure to put everything you're keeping in your craft room in clearly labelled bags/boxes that will stay in the room. Once you've cleared this path take a moment to pat yourself on the back, and say

'I love myself' from the bottom of your heart. You are doing *such* a good job!

Now let's make the path wider. Pick the side of the path closest to the door or the workstation, and start clearing the floor making this side wider and wider. Celebrate every time you get all the way to a wall! When you've cleared floor space from the path to the wall, stop, love yourself, and think a bit about how you'll be using this room:

Will you be working just at one place, and using the rest of the room for storage? A knitter may need a comfortable chair with good lighting and a table for resting a few things on, and then access to storage.

Will you be working in various areas depending on what stage of crafting you're in? A quilter may have different areas in the room for cutting, piecing and sewing, plus storage.

Think about how to arrange the room so you can easily move from one area to another, and you can store the things you need close to where you'll be using them. You may want to tape up some signs or some sticky notes to remind yourself where you'll be doing different things, and what you'll be storing there.

Now you can start setting up your space while you continue to love your clutter away. So when you come across something that belongs in a certain area in your room *and* you can put it away there right away, go ahead. Don't dig out things that are already in a 'Use it' box though – you can put these things away at the end.

So, you've got a clear path from the door to the workspace, a clear workspace, a clear path to your closet/shelf/storage, and some clear floor space. Wonderful!! I hope you're getting excited about working on projects in your shiny new craft room!!

Let's clear the rest of the floor now. Make sure you have all your labelled bags/boxes ready for garbage, recycling, extras/donate, illegal tenants, use it, wrong room and IDK, plus your two clear bins if you're including a second craft in your room. Work your way from the edge of the path towards the wall, sorting one item at a time into its best category. Whenever a bag/box is full take it to its home. Remember that your 'Use it' items are staying in the room to be put away when you're done clearing the room.

Once the floor is clear, work to sort through each additional area. This probably includes places like closets, shelves, and dressers. Try to be really honest with yourself about which things you'll actually use in your crafting, and which items you *really* might like, but have no actual use for. Donate everything you won't be using. You'll find that having a clear space will clear your mind for peaceful creating in your craft room – well worth it!

How are you doing? Take a break whenever you need as long as you leave the area safe, put sorted things in your home, and love yourself for at least three minutes before you end any clutter-clearing session.

Now it's time to start setting up your room! If you haven't put up signs about where you want to store different supplies in your room, do it now. Don't worry about getting too specific, just give yourself some general guidelines to go by.

Start with the big items – cutting pads, sewing machine, ironing board and iron, etc. Put them in an easy-to-get-at space, or, if it's something you'll be using regularly, set it where it will be used.

Next, find a good place for your current project (if you have one. If not, move to the next paragraph.) Setting this up may give you ideas about where you want things to be kept. Feel free to change your signs and be flexible about your set up. You're aiming for 'good' here, not 'perfect'. Nothing kills creativity faster than trying for perfection.

Now you can start unpacking the boxes/bags of 'Use it' and putting things away. Use lots of sticky notes to label what you're putting where. Think of this like Christmas – all those supplies are little gifts for you to enjoy! *Except* when you exceed your space. When you run out of room to put things away, have another sort, and only keep the very very best most useful supplies.

Choosing to keep only what you have room for is one of the most important parts of setting up a usable space. Let's face it, there's an unlimited amount of craft supplies that you'd love to have. And tomorrow you may see something else that you really want. So make space, leave room, and enjoy your hobby.

If you decide to buy some containers to put supplies in, be sure to buy clear containers with lids that are easy to open and close. And then label each one. This will really help you find what you need quickly, and put things away easily.

Your craft room is done when you've sorted through everything in it and put the things you're keeping into homes with labels. If you're going to regularly be working on a project it's OK to keep the supplies out and available for use. Otherwise keep everything except oversized items stored in labeled containers.

Take everything that does not belong in your craft room out and put it where it belongs.

You did it! You cleaned out your craft room, and set up and organized space to use! A big congratulations to you!

WRONG ROOM AND IDK

Wow! Can you believe how much progress you've made? Way to go! I hope you can feel me smiling at you through the pages, because all the work you've done to love your clutter away is *really* impressive!

Now it's time to take care of those Wrong Room and IDK boxes/bags. Let's start with the Wrong Room items.

Get yourself set up somewhere with some space – maybe the floor in your livingroom or your kitchen table. Grab a bag/box and label it 'Donate' and make sure you also have bags for garbage and recycling. It may have been a while since you set aside these Wrong Room items, and I have a feeling your priorities have shifted a bit.

See, when someone really commits to loving their clutter away (like you have), they start to have different requirements for what to keep and what to take away. It's really neat how you begin to change your thoughts, and keep less than you used to want to keep. Now, as you sort through these Wrong Room items, you'll find more things to donate, toss, or recycle. Which means your home will have <u>even less</u> clutter – fantastic!

Sort through your Wrong Room things one at a time, putting them in donate, garbage, recycle, or which room they belong in. Make labels for each room so that you don't lose track of your sorting system. When your pile/bag/box gets bigger, take a break and go put the things in their right room *and* where they belong in that room. If you don't have space to <u>easily</u> put them away, you'll need to do a bit of a sort to decide what you'll keep. Remember, you only have the space you have, and shoving, squishing or squeezing things into a space just makes it harder to put things away, harder to find things, and harder to keep your spaces tidy. Only keep what you can comfortable put away.

Once you've put the Wrong Room items away in their right room, come back to your sorting area and keep going. If you start to feel anxious or overwhelmed, take some deep breaths, and spend 3 minutes saying 'I love myself' with your eyes closed.

When the Wrong Room items are all put away, do something to celebrate! You're doing amazing!

Now let's take a look at those IDK items. Again, have a bag/box ready for Donate, as well as garbage and recycling. Sort the items one at a time, either into donate, garbage, or recycling, or to the room they belong in. Since these are things you weren't sure what to do with, you'll probably still have things you just don't know about. Leave these things in their own pile, and take care of everything you can make a decision about.

Put all the things away that you can. As always, if things don't fit in their home, you'll need to love things away until your most important 'Keep' items are safely stored.

Now let's take a look at the remaining IDK items. Pick up the thing closest to you, and answer this question:

What is it for?

If you answer 'I don't know', then donate/toss it. If you don't know what it's for, and you haven't needed it the whole time you've been loving your clutter away, then you can let it go.

If you have a specific purpose for it, then ask yourself:

Where will I use this?

Put it in this place if there's room. If there isn't room... you guessed it! Have a little sort and keep only the things that fit where they should.

If the item has sentimental meaning then ask yourself:

How does it make me feel?

If it brings up *any* bad feelings, then love yourself lots and let it go. Your home is the place for love, joy, and peace. Any things that do not contribute to this do not belong in your home. (Note: this policy generally doesn't apply to *people* living in your home – but it's something to consider!)

If it brings up happy or loving feelings, then choose to place it somewhere where it's clear that you value it, and you can enjoy looking at it. If you don't have room anywhere for it, then you need to sort through your treasures, and keep only the best that you have room for.

Each item in your IDK gets this same treatment. If it's special enough, give it a place of honor in your home. If it's not special, and doesn't serve an important purpose then love it away.

Well done! The IDK items are often the trickiest to deal with, and you've succeeded! You rock!

DEALING WITH THE STUFF FROM
THE PAST

At this point you're making loving yourself a priority, and you understand how loving yourself changes everything about how you see things, and being able to let go of things. You're also building skills in sorting, decision making, and organizing. When it comes to things from the past you get to use all of these skills to face the job, bring closure where you need it, and remind yourself what really matters.

Many people hang onto things from the past for a few different reasons:

1. They miss the past and wish they could go back to the way things were
2. They have regrets about the past which cause a lot of negative feelings
3. They feel obligated to keep things from the past

Missing the Past:

If you're missing the past, first take 3 minutes to love yourself. Next, take a few minutes to write down some of your best memories from the past. Then, write down some of the good things that are part of your life right now. Finally, write down some things you are looking forward to, or would like to enjoy in the future.

Begin to sort through your things from the past, looking for a few things that will bring up the good memories you wrote about. Choose things that you will be happy to display, and won't over-whelm your space. Put these things on display right away – I'll bet they look really nice, and bring a smile to your face. (If they don't make you smile, try again to pick some 'happy memory items'.)

Finish sorting through these things, and keep aside one container of things to keep stored. Make sure the container is clearly labelled – even better if the container itself is clear. Let go of the rest of the things. You've done right by displaying a few things, and keeping a few things. Now it's time to focus on enjoying the life you are living right now, and making new memories.

Regrets About the Past:

If you're struggling with regrets, this will really interfere with your ability to sort through things from the past. Probably you want to avoid it all because it brings up such negative feelings. Your skills in loving yourself are going to help you through this. Take 3 minutes to love yourself. Really focus on meaning it, and feeling that love all the way through your body.

I can't change your past, and neither can you. But you can begin to work on loving the person you were in the past – even though you don't like the things that happened. That person you were needs to be loved and forgiven. Nothing else will help you more now than loving and forgiving. As you begin to sort through the things from the past, spend a lot of time saying 'I love myself' when you think about the past. Then, picture that loved person who you were being slowly and peacefully let go into a comfortable, safe place.

Take all the time you need to sort your things, so that you can continue this process whenever you need. Keep things that bring back any happy memories, and release the rest. Even though this may take a while, stick to it. Whether it takes a few long hours, or a few long days, working through these things with a thoughtful and caring outlook is going to make such a difference. You won't have to dread going through these things anymore, because it will be done. Ahhhh…doesn't that feel better? Good for you. This is an amazing journey you're choosing to take towards a better day tomorrow, and every day after. You *are* loved, and you *are* forgiven.

Obligated to Keep Things:

Clutterers are *really nice* people who are always thinking of others. In fact, they're so concerned with what others might want/need that their homes are filled with things for other people. Especially things from the past.

This might be you if you've keep all your (now adult) child's school things, the contents of your grandma's house, everything from that time your parents downsized, and the crafts the lady down the street made for you and your sister when you were in primary school.

Perhaps you weren't exactly *asked* to keep all this for everyone else but you're certain they'd be really upset if you got rid of it. Or maybe everyone *does* ask you to keep things for them, because they know you will. And because they really don't want all that stuff filling up their tidy, organized homes…

What's really going on here is that you're giving love, time, and space to clutter, and you're not loving yourself. Quite frankly, the people you're holding clutter for are not loving you either. These may even be the same people that are always on your case to clean up your stuff!

The solution starts with loving yourself – of course! So take some time to do this, and love yourself <u>unconditionally</u>. Because loving yourself does *not* require you to put your own home at risk for others. Just the opposite! Loving yourself means having a safe, warm, and welcoming home that reflects <u>you, your life, and your future</u>. You do *not* need to be someone else's free storage unit!

There's just one more thing to cover before we look at *how* to love these things away. Some of you say you're keeping things for others, but it's not really true. You're keeping them because it's too hard for you to let them go. Maybe your kids have already told you they don't want their old school things, and they don't want grandma's dish set, but *you* just don't want to let those things go.

So, take some slow breaths, and then take 3 minutes to say 'I love myself'. Now you can start to work through this by being totally honest. Are you keeping these things from the past because *you* want to? There's no judgement against you if you are! You are still loved, valuable and important! Just allow yourself to be completely truthful about what you're feeling with these things from the past.

OK, now let's do something about these things! First task – love yourself! Next task, sort these things from the past into two piles: 1. Things people have specifically asked you to keep for them, and 2. Things you have not been asked to keep for people – remember, you're free to be completely honest here.

Of the things people have asked you to keep, take out anything for people you have regular contact with, you are confident these things are treasured by them, *and* you have room to <u>safely and easily store them</u>. If your daughter has always loved grandma's dish set, but she's backpacking in Europe right now and can't keep it with her, it makes sense for you to store it for her. If your ex-sister-in-law hasn't spoken to you in 5 years and you're keeping the wedding present she gave you in case she wants it back, it *doesn't love yourself* to keep it.

If you do identify any things you are keeping for others because they've asked you to, take a few minutes to check with each of them that they do still want those things, and that they have a plan for when they'll collect them from you. (If they won't ever be collecting them, then there's no point in keeping them – make sure they know this.) Take any things you are still keeping, pack them up safely with labels that say who they are for and what's in them, and store them out of your way. Well done!

Now you get to really love yourself! Because removing things that drag you down – like other people's stuff – is really liberating! Let's look at pile #2 – things you have not been asked to keep for people. Sort these into three piles: donate, wishful keeping (things you actually wish to keep for yourself), and IDK. The IDK is things you feel very strongly you need to check with people about before you donate them.

When you take the things you've sorted into donate, and donate them, you're showing your commitment to love yourself, and create good, healing space in your home. So go ahead, and get those donate items to their new home at the thrift store. Remember **TIP #1** If you are donating things at a thrift store or charity shop *do not* go in and look around. *Do not* put a single thing back in your car. Make this a rule that you always follow.

Next, make a list of the IDK items and who you will be talking to about them. Decide on a reasonable time frame for you to hold on to this thing for you. (Reasonable means short.) And then go call them. Be very clear that you feel you should be keeping these items for the person you're talking to, and you need to know if that's how they feel. Of course, if they say they *don't* want them, you're off the hook! And if they really do want them, ask them when is the <u>soonest</u> they can come collect them. If it's a reasonable time (a few days to a month), then confirm with them that they will come, and note what they've committed to.

If they do not give a time frame, you can ask them if they'll pay to ship it. This is a nice way of finding out if they really want this item. If they're still being vague, you will need to ask outright 'is this something you truly want?' Be clear that you're working very hard to create a safe home for yourself, and you can't store things for them anymore.

Remember a while ago when I said that clutterers were really nice people? You first of all need to be really nice to yourself! And that means making sure you're not being treated like a doormat, or someone obligated to fill their house for someone else's benefit, or a free storage unit. Since you already have a time frame in mind of how long you're able to hold it for them, if they can't work with this, then you can let them know that you'll donate it after this time. This is a great opportunity to see how much this person values *you* over the things you're holding for them.

Here's the bottom line:

Tip #22 You do not need to keep things indefinitely for someone else. If they won't make arrangements to collect it, it's not that important to them. The first few times it may feel really hard to love those things away. But once you've communicated about these things, and given some time for them to be collected the most loving thing you can do for yourself is to let those things go. Love yourself lots, and look for relationships where you're valued for being you, not for keeping things.

Last pile! Time to take a look at those wishful things – the items you wish you could keep, whether you have a reason or not. After dealing with all those things you were keeping for others, is there anything here you can love away now? You're probably starting to think that clutter is a lot of work. You're right. Managing our clutter gets in the way of living! So, take a quick sort through the pile, pulling out the things you'll let go of. Well done!

Next, are there things that are really beautiful, or make you smile? If there are, do you have a place where you could display them now? Go ahead, and put these things out so you can enjoy them! If you don't have room, you can always make room by loving away some clutter. This is a work in progress, where you're always doing things to make your home more warm and inviting, so switching things up, and letting go of things is a great thing to do.

You're doing great! You've found the best items in your wishful pile, and given them a special place in your home. Now, every time you walk by them you can smile and say 'I sure do love myself'. The rest of the things in the pile can now be loved right out of your home. Pack them up, pat yourself on the back, and take them away. *You* have done absolutely amazing!!

WELCOME TO THE BEGINNING

T*hank you* for sticking with this book until the end! If you've just been reading it through, now you know the whole process in your head, and you can translate that to action. Please, please give the techniques here a try. You don't have to believe that they'll work, you don't even have to believe in yourself. You just have to start loving yourself and take the very first piece of clutter and sort it. Keep going, and find out what the big deal is about loving your clutter away! I'm cheering you on through every step!

If you're now the proud resident of a less cluttered home, I don't even have words to say how incredibly proud I am of you. Through the years, I've worked with many clutterers and I know it's not easy to tackle your clutter, but you've done it!!

More than anything else, I want this book to have you loving yourself for the rest of your life. Keep up the practice of taking time every day to say 'I love myself'. Do it in the bathroom, when you're walking, during commercials, whenever you pass by a thrift store, or see a FREE sign. Always, always, always love yourself, OK?

There's a few more ways to keep up with all the progress you've made:

- Keep a bag in the front closet, or somewhere convenient to put "donate" items in as you come across them. You will always be finding things you no longer use, no longer need, or no longer like. Immediately pop those into your donate bag, get rid of that bag when it's full, and replace it with another empty bag.
- Practice having a tidy time each day. Just take 10 minutes to grab things that are outside their homes, and put them away. You don't have to do it all, just keep on putting things away.
- Be a loving shopper. Always love yourself before you enter any store. Remember all the work you put into loving your clutter away and make sure the things you purchase will not interfere with your beautiful uncluttered space.
- Consistently take things away when you add things. If you buy a package of socks, get rid of all the holey worn-out socks. Clean out your fridge before you buy groceries. Toss some grubby shirts when you buy a new one. You always want your things to become lighter (less) instead of heavier (more).

Making such a huge change has taken a lot of time and effort. You'll still need to put some effort into sorting, loving clutter away, and cleaning your home. These are *not* tasks that go away. But now you have the skills to deal with them, and the space to manage the things you have.

Now you have a big decision to make: what's next? You've spent a good part of your life feeling obligated to your clutter. You may have avoided commitments and opportunities because you felt you should be at home with your clutter. You may have shied away from having people over, and getting close to people because you couldn't welcome them into your home. That's all changed now — how wonderful!

So, let's start to fill some of your time with things that really matter. If you have friends or family with/near you, start spending time with them in your home and around town. Find simple pleasures to enjoy together. Maybe even invite your neighbor over for a coffee or a beer. You can do that now!

Look for ways to do meaningful things. There are lots of places and people that would love to have you around. Try a few. Look for somewhere that has a positive environment, where you can do something that will leave you feeling fulfilled. However, watch out for places where you'll have access to free/cheap things. Volunteering at thrift stores is not an option for clutterers—even those who have done such a fantastic job at loving their clutter away!

Along those lines, be careful not to fill your time with things that involve, well... things. Convert your old shopping buddy to a walking buddy. Avoid discount stores, yard sales, and any other places where you will have to work against your affinity for all things clutterish. Instead, look for productive, healthy ways to spend your time.

This is your real beginning. I promise you that you can create an amazing life and keep a calm, uncluttered home at the same time! Just love yourself first, last, and all the time in the middle too.

One more thing: Please take a minute to leave a review for *Love Your Clutter Away!*

Happy Decluttering,

Carmen

GLOSSARY OF CLUTTER TERMS

Garbage – anything that has served its purpose, anything that will not be used and cannot be recycled or donated, anything that no longer functions properly (things, not people...),

Recycling – varies by area. Anything that can easily be dropped off/picked up to be turned into another useful product. The key word here is <u>easily</u>. I once worked with a client who was saving all their VHS tapes to be recycled – at a location that was a 3.5 hour drive away. This is not easy, therefore the VHS tapes were garbage.

Illegal Tenants – items you've been holding in your home that belong to someone else (often family). If they don't pay rent and they don't belong to you they're illegal tenants and must be evicted.

Wrong Room – the category used in sorting for things you come across that belong in another room.

Use It – the category used in sorting for items that will remain in the room you are currently working in.

IDK – short for I Don't Know. The category used in sorting for items you just can't make a decision about right now.

TIPS

TIP #1 If you are donating things at a thrift store or charity shop *do not* go in and look around. *Do not* put a single thing back in your car. Make this a rule that you always follow.

TIP #2 Don't wait until you have 'enough' or a full load of anything you're getting rid of. You will be more successful getting 3 things gone this week than saving 200 things to get rid of next year.

TIP #3 When you come across paperwork, your main task is to separate the urgent from the mountain(s). Urgent means you must deal with it or face serious consequences. Bills are urgent. Coupons are not urgent. Legal summons are urgent. Newsletters are not urgent. Place the urgent items in a visible container that will ONLY hold urgent paperwork. Place the rest of the paperwork in a box labelled 'papers' or something similar that makes sense to you. (Don't worry, I'll help you out with all that paperwork later in the book.)

TIP #4 When you feel like you can't keep on going (or just really don't want to) find something in your space that belongs somewhere else, and get up and take it there.

TIP #5 When you are returning an item to its home (or closer to its home if you can't get all the way there) do not stop, do not pass go, but go <u>straight back</u> to where you were working.

Tip #6 Watch out for the rest of the world. When you've cleared a small space, *you* know you've done a great thing, and *I* know you've done a great thing, but the rest of the world won't know. If you share your home with others, they probably won't be impressed with your new, clear small space. They might even be a bit of a downer. But <u>you know</u> it's a big deal, and you *must* congratulate yourself and keep on going!

Tip #7 ASK PEOPLE if they want things you've been keeping for them, and respect them if they don't. You do not become more valuable by hoarding things others might want. You learn to value yourself by loving yourself.

Tip #8 Retraining other people. Some people in your life may be used to viewing you as their free storage unit. You will need to retrain them, just like you are retraining yourself! Let them know you are changing how you manage the house, and can no longer store their things. If they care enough about their things, they'll arrange to collect them.

Tip #9 It's good to donate, but only donate good stuff!

TIP #10 At any time if you are feeling like you just can't do anymore, remember that it's OK to stop. You're doing something that's very different than what you're used to and it can take some time to get in the groove. Always end a loving your clutter away session by taking three minutes to say 'I love myself' out loud. Then, make sure the area you were working on is left safe, take all your sorted categories to their homes, and give yourself a well-deserved break!

TIP #11 Every time you set aside a box of things you've sorted, label it clearly with a label that is certain to stay with the box. That way, when you come across it again you'll remember what it is and where it came from. You'll be surprised how much duplicate sorting this little task will save you!

TIP #12 Things that have been taking up space in your home for so long that they have changed color/quality have overstayed their welcome and are clutter, not useful. Throw them out.

TIP #13 – If you've had food so that it has passed its expiry date than you've got more food than you eat in a reasonable time. Toss it, and buy smaller amounts of food that you *can* consume in a reasonable time.

TIP #14 A sale (for food or anything else) is not a bargain if it's too much to manage. Avoid buying things that will pile up in your home.

TIP #15 If you share your home with others, it's inevitable that you're going to come across clutter that they created. Be very careful not to build resentment when this happens. Everyone you live with is human and needs to be loved. This is the most important. Even more important than loving your clutter away!

Tip #16 Your house isn't a storage unit. No matter how expensive something was, if it's not usable and wonderful *to you* it needs to go. If your first reason for keeping something is how much it cost, that's a sign that it's not something you need to keep.

Tip #17 You are always making progress if:

- Things are leaving your house
- You are not replacing the things that leave your house AND
- Things are making their way to their Rightful Room in your home

TIP #18 If you *do* find gifts you bought and forgot at any time during your sorting, make sure you label them who you bought them for. Then, place a reminder in your phone or in your calendar for 3 weeks before you would give it to them. (For example, if you found Christmas gifts, put a reminder in your phone at the beginning of December that says 'Christmas gifts are under the spare room bed (or wherever they are)' or 'Mother's Day gift is in closet'. Choose one place in your home to store gifts, and label every one with whom it's for. Never buy a gift unless it is intended for someone specific.

TIP #19 Your name and address are *not* private or sensitive information! It's in the public domain, and there is no benefit to you in shredding papers that only have your name and address. Don't waste time shredding papers only because your name and address are on them.

TIP #20 Any organizing system only works if it works for <u>YOU</u>. When you choose categories or labels, pick the first word that comes to mind. This is most likely to be the word that you will think of first the next time you're looking for your item. For example, 'Vehicle', 'Car', 'Toyota', and 'Mindy' (or whatever you name your car) all mean the same thing, but only one of them will be the right label for things related to your car.

Tip #21 Managing paperwork

- Open all your mail every day. Immediately recycle junk and unnecessary papers.
- Separate critical paperwork from general paperwork. Any critical paperwork that can be easily dealt with can be handled right away and then sent to the general paperwork pile.
- Keep a highlighter where you open mail. Highlight due dates and action points.
- Regularly file your general paperwork. The more often you file it, the less time it will take.
- Twice a year go through every paper in your files. This is a quick pass through to find things that are no longer necessary and remove them. I once heard someone refer to this as 'grooming' your files. It's just like getting a little trim to keep things tidy. Choose times of the year that are not as busy, and that make sense to you, and then put a reminder on your phone and in your calendar.

Tip #21 You are NOT obligated to finish everything you start. Get rid of projects that are not a good fit for your current life. This includes projects that are too difficult, expired (baby toys for your now-teenager), make you feel guilty every time you look at them, or you just don't want to do.

Tip #22 You do not need to keep things indefinitely for someone else. If they won't make arrangements to collect it, it's not that important to them.

ALSO BY CARMEN KLASSEN

NON FICTION

Love Your Clutter Away

Before Your Parents Move In

* * *

SUCCESS ON HER TERMS

Book 1: Sweet, Smart, and Struggling

Book 2: The Cost of Caring

Book 3: Life Upcycled

Book 4: Heartwarming Designs (preorder)

Book 5: A Roof Over Their Heads (coming soon)

Made in the USA
Middletown, DE
17 January 2020

83369980R00084